SHAKESPEARE MADE EASY

MODERN ENGLISH VERSION
SIDE-BY-SIDE WITH FULL ORIGINAL TEXT

As You Like It

EDITED AND RENDERED INTO MODERN ENGLISH BY
Gayle Holste

BARRON'S

All inquiries should be addressed to:
Barron's Educational Series, Inc.
250 Wireless Boulevard
Hauppauge, NY 11788
www.barronseduc.com

Library of Congress Catalog Card No. 2008042447

ISBN-13: 978-0-7641-4272-7
ISBN-10: 0-7641-4272-0

Library of Congress Cataloging-in-Publication Data

Shakespeare, William, 1564–1616.
   As you like it / edited and rendered into modern English by Gayle Holste.
     p. cm.—(Shakespeare made easy)
   "Modern English version side-by-side with full original text."
   Includes bibiliographical references.
   ISBN-13: 978-0-7641-4272-7
   ISBN-10: 0-7641-4272-0
   1. Father and daughters—Drama. 2. Exiles—Drama. 3. Shakespeare,
William, 1564–1616. As you like it. I. Holste, Gayle. II. Title.
   PR2803.A2H58   2009
   822.3'3—dc22   2008042447

Contents

Introduction

Shakespeare Made Easy is designed to help those who struggle with Shakespeare's language read his plays with greater ease and comprehension. William Shakespeare wrote his plays to appeal to a wide audience, but in the approximately four hundred years since the plays were written, the English language has undergone significant changes. Consequently, although Shakespeare is regarded by many as the greatest playwright in the English language, readers often find the language barrier insurmountable. Even though it is possible, with practice, to read the plays in the original language, many find the task too difficult and give up either in disgust or despair. Footnotes are helpful, but they can interrupt the flow of the language, and many readers become so discouraged with having to refer to footnotes that they simply give up.

Shakespeare Made Easy offers a helping hand not only to those who want to get better acquainted with Shakespeare's plays for their own sake but also to those who are required to study the plays but find the task of deciphering the language overwhelming. Of course, there is no substitute for reading and studying the plays themselves in Shakespeare's own words. The unmatched beauty of the language can never be duplicated, but the modern version will assist the reader in distinguishing between the characters and in understanding what is happening in the play.

There are a number of possible ways to use *Shakespeare Made Easy*. One option is to read the play in the original language, referring to the modern version only when necessary. Another possibility is to read the entire play in the modern version to know what is going on and then to read the original with this knowledge firmly in mind. The bracketed notations concerning the ways in which lines may be spoken by an actor—although giving only one of the possible interpretations—can be especially helpful. If the reader plans to view a filmed version of the play, reading the modern version in advance can help overcome the difficulty of trying to understand the spoken language, as well.

Whichever method you use, *Shakespeare Made Easy* will prove a valuable resource for your study of the play. It is not intended as a substitute for the original play, since even the most careful "translation" of the text will lose certain aspects such as poetic meter, alliteration, and verbal humor.

Whether you are studying the play for a class or reading it for enjoyment or to increase your acquaintance with Shakespeare's works, the Activities section at the end of the book will be helpful in pointing out themes or issues that may have escaped your notice as you read. If you need to write a paper about this play, this section will help you generate topic ideas. It will also help you as you write the paper to make sure that you have correctly interpreted a quote you are using in support of one of your points.

Using *Shakespeare Made Easy* will pave your way to a far better understanding of and appreciation for Shakespeare's plays and will remove the textual difficulties that may have caused you to stumble in past attempts. Not only will you gain confidence in discussing the plot and characters of the play, but you will also develop a greater awareness of the ways in which Shakespeare used language for poetic expression as well as for raising intriguing and challenging moral and philosophical issues.

Ever since the works of William Shakespeare entered the canon of English literature, they have excited the admiration of generations of scholars, readers, and theatergoers. Even if you've had negative experiences in the past with Shakespeare's plays—in fact, especially if you've had negative experiences—you will find yourself pleasantly surprised at just how entertaining his plays can be. We're glad you've chosen *Shakespeare Made Easy* as a companion on your journey to a better understanding of the plays of William Shakespeare.

William Shakespeare

His Life

Considering the impact that William Shakespeare has had on English literature, surprisingly little is known about his life. We do know that he was born to a prominent wool and leather merchant and his wife in 1564 (the actual day is in doubt but tradition sets it at April 23) in Stratford-upon-Avon, England. He is believed to have been educated at the local grammar school, although no lists of pupils survive from the sixteenth century. He did not attend university.

We also know from parish records that he married Anne Hathaway in 1582 when he was eighteen and she was twenty-six. They had three children; Susanna was their eldest, followed by twins, Judith and Hamnet. Their son, Hamnet, died at the age of about eleven, but the two daughters, Susanna and Judith, reached adulthood.

There are many stories about Shakespeare's life, such as the one alleging that he fled Stratford after having been caught poaching deer in the park belonging to Sir Thomas Lucy, a local justice of the peace. Like the rest of the tales about Shakespeare during this period of his life, this story cannot be verified and is probably untrue. Because his plays demonstrate extensive knowledge about a variety of subjects, articles have been written "proving" that Shakespeare must have temporarily pursued a career in either law, botany, or medicine or spent time as a soldier or sailor, to name a few of the occupations that he is speculated to have had.

The truth is, we simply don't know for sure what Shakespeare did for a living in the ten years following his marriage to Anne Hathaway. Ordinarily, as the eldest son he would have been expected to take over his father's business, but again there is no evidence to show that he did (or, for that matter, did not) serve an apprenticeship to his father. He may have spent some time with a traveling troupe of actors, but, aside from the baptismal records for his children, we have no actual records about him from the time of his marriage to Hathaway until 1592, by which time he had left Stratford and traveled to London. His wife and children remained in Stratford.

The next documented evidence pertaining to Shakespeare comes in 1592, when Shakespeare received his first critical recognition. It came in the form of a petulant outburst by fellow playwright Robert Greene who, apparently annoyed by the attention being received by this newcomer, complained bitterly in a pamphlet written from his deathbed about the "upstart crow . . . Shake-scene."

From about 1594 onward, Shakespeare was associated with a new theatrical company, The Lord Chamberlain's Men; by 1599 Shakespeare had become a shareholder in the company. The troupe gave command performances for Queen Elizabeth I as well as her successor, King James I. After King James' accession to the throne, the troupe took the name "The King's Men."

The King's Men performed at *The Globe* theater, which they owned. Of course, *The Globe* was not the only theater in London. *The Curtain* (built in 1577) and *The Rose* (1587), as well as a number of other theaters, also provided entertainment to the citizens. In addition to these open-air "public" theaters, there were many "private" or indoor theaters. Shakespeare and his friends purchased one of the private theaters, *The Blackfriars*, which was giving them especially stiff competition because of the popularity of the child actors who performed there.

With so many theaters in operation, the demand for plays was high. Shakespeare may have earned a living for a time by reworking older plays and by collaborating with others on new ones, and of course he also wrote his own plays. In addition to the uncertainty about many facts pertaining to his life, there even is debate about the exact number of plays Shakespeare wrote; some say he wrote thirty-seven, others say thirty-eight.

Shakespeare stopped writing for the stage in about 1611, and, having prospered not only from his writing but also from his shares in the theatrical company, he retired to Stratford, where he installed his family in New Place, one of the more expensive homes in Stratford. He died at the age of fifty-two on April 23, 1616.

His Plays

Many people are surprised to learn that none of the original handwritten manuscripts of Shakespeare's plays survives. At that time, plays were not considered to be "literature" in the same way that poetry was. In fact, when Shakespeare wrote his plays, they would have been the property of the producing company, which was concerned, not with publication of the plays, but with producing them on stage. The company would have bought them for about ten pounds apiece, and when a play finished its theatrical run and the copies were of no further use to the company, they often were discarded.

Roughly half of Shakespeare's plays were published during his lifetime in quarto (17 centimeters by 21 centimeters) volumes, although many of these were pirated copies. Booksellers often would hire someone to take shorthand notes during a performance, and then they would sell these unauthorized copies. This method for acquiring a copy of the play, needless to say, could result in numerous errors depending on the accuracy of the transcriber. In other instances of piracy, actors' scripts were purchased by a bookseller after the play had completed its run, but since each actor's copy would contain only his scenes, the actor would have to provide the rest of the text from memory, which often proved faulty. These pirated copies are referred to as "bad" Quartos. Even when a printer was working from a good manuscript (probably a prompt copy obtained from the theater), mistakes often contaminated the printed copy. In addition to all these problems, portions of the plays were sometimes censored for a variety of reasons, resulting in still further corruption of the text.

Fortunately, seven years after Shakespeare's death an authoritative version of his works, the First Folio (21 centimeters by 34 centimeters), edited by two of his theatrical partners and fellow actors, John Hemming and Henry Condell, was published: They claimed in the introduction to have used his original manuscripts, but that claim is unverified. The First Folio contained thirty-six of his plays and was titled *Comedies, Histories, and Tragedies*. Despite the Folio's apparent superiority to other printings of Shakespeare's plays, serious questions remain, and debate continues concerning discrepancies between the various early editions.

Because of the discrepancies between different editions of the plays, when one of Shakespeare's plays is published, editors must make decisions about which version to use. Often, the edition will contain lines from several of the oldest texts, but since in some cases there remains significant disagreement about which text is the "best" or most accurate, the reader may discover that there are differences between editions of the play. Many editions include notes at the end of the play to indicate the words or lines that have an alternate reading.

His Theater

In Elizabethan times, the London authorities viewed playgoing as both morally and politically questionable; they also believed that the large crowds that attended the plays created an increased risk for spreading the bubonic plague. In fact, the playhouses were closed twice during Shakespeare's lifetime as a result of outbreaks of the plague. Because of the hostile atmosphere created by the civil authorities, playhouses were typically built outside the city limits in order to place them beyond the jurisdiction of authorities.

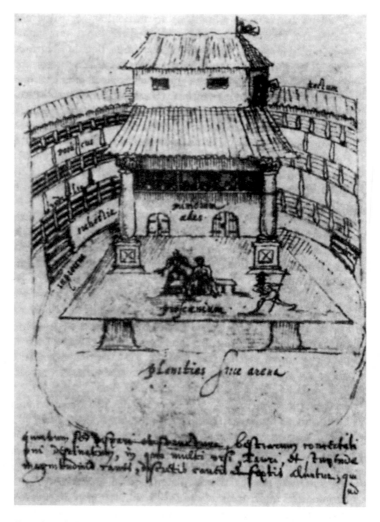

Interior of the Swan Theatre—from a pen and ink drawing made in 1596 (Mansell Collection)

When The Lord Chamberlain's Men (the troupe to which Shakespeare belonged), first began performing, *The Theater*, owned by Richard and Cuthbert Burbage, was their theatrical home. Constructed in 1576 just outside the city limits of London, *The Theater* was the first of the public playhouses. Plays had previously been performed in England in the square- or rectangular-shaped yards of the inns where traveling bands of actors stayed, but this arrangement had a serious drawback—it was far too easy for customers to enter and leave the grounds without paying the price of admission. Playhouses like *The Theater* were therefore a significant improvement since the enclosed design made it possible to have a single opening where tickets could be taken from those entering.

The Lord Chamberlain's Men were financially successful, but a problem arose in 1598 concerning the property on which *The Theater* stood. The owner of the property planned to have the playhouse torn down once the lease on the land expired, so in late 1598 the Lord Chamberlain's Men dismantled the building and reassembled it a short distance from the south bank of the River Thames, renaming it *The Globe*.

In 1603, The Lord Chamberlain's Men regrouped under the patronage of King James I and took the name The King's Men; the shareholders were thenceforward considered to be members of the royal household. Unfortunately, the company's fortunes took a downturn in 1613 when, during a performance of *Henry VIII*, a cannon was fired, setting the thatched roof of *The Globe* ablaze. Within an hour, the building was destroyed.

The King's Men rebuilt the playhouse, and the new *The Globe* theater, completed in 1614, was circular in shape. The "wooden O" (as it is referred to in *Henry V*) of *The Globe* actually had twenty sides, with an outer diameter of about one hundred yards. Some historians have estimated that it could hold up to three thousand people, but others dispute that figure as being far too high.

Playbills would be posted around the city to advertise for new plays, but due to the fact that the roofs of "public" theaters such as *The Globe* were open to the elements, plays could be performed only in daylight and in good weather. The theatrical company would fly a flag from the roof of the building to notify people if a performance was to proceed. If, however, the flag was not flown, theatergoers would be spared an unnecessary trip.

Those attending a play paid the gatekeeper at the entrance. In addition to standing room around the stage, seats were available in the three tiers of the gallery which encircled the playhouse. For the price of one penny (about sixty cents today), the "groundlings," as they were called, gained admission to the pit. Those who could afford to do so paid for gallery seating; the lowest tier was the least expensive, with the price climbing to as high as one shilling (about seven dollars today) for seats in the uppermost tier. The roof shielded the patrons seated in the galleries either from the heat of the sun or, in case the weather turned bad, from a sudden downpour.

Plays typically had a theatrical run of ten performances, although, depending on the popularity of the piece, some were performed up to about sixteen times; less popular plays, however, might have only six performances. The performances proceeded without intermission and usually took about two hours, although a number of Shakespeare's plays run significantly longer. When the play was about to begin, a trumpet would sound three times.

Shakespeare's plays were performed on what is referred to as a "thrust" stage; it was about five feet high and measured $27\frac{1}{2}$ feet deep by 43 feet wide; it probably sloped downward at the front (downstage) and projected out into the pit. The stage was covered by a roof (referred to as "the heavens"), which was painted to resemble a starlit sky upon which the signs of the zodiac were depicted. The area beneath the stage was referred to as "hell"; a trapdoor in the floor of the stage allowed for the entrances and exits of ghosts, monsters, and devils.

There was no scenery, nor was there a curtain that could be closed at the end of scenes or acts, so playwrights used the lines spoken by the actors to set the scene and to indicate when a scene or act was ending. A rhyming couplet, for example, would often indicate the conclusion of a scene. The gallery directly behind the stage was used for scenes in which actors were required to be either in an upper story of a house, on the battlements of a castle, or in some other elevated position. Musicians and even spectators also occupied the gallery.

At the rear of the stage (upstage) was the "tiring house" where the actors dressed (attired themselves). The tiring house had two or three doors providing access to the stage. Even though many of the plays performed were set in earlier times, the actors did not wear period costumes; the period in which a play was set would merely be suggested by certain period touches in the costumes, such as spears or helmets. Consequently, a play such as *Julius Caesar*, which was set around 44 B.C.E., would have been performed in the current fashions of Elizabethan England. However, despite being historically inaccurate, the costumes the actors wore were quite lavish and were therefore not a disappointment to the audience.

Since it was illegal for women to perform in public at that time, boys or young men played the women's roles in the plays. Often, in order for a boy actor to be tall enough to be convincing in the role of an adult woman, he had to wear chopines (wooden platforms strapped to the soles of the shoes); the long skirts, which were fashionable, hid the chopines from view. Because of the restriction on women performing, Shakespeare's plays had few female characters, and, in many of his plays, the heroine would spend much of the play disguised as a boy.

The plays of Shakespeare were of course crucial to the success of the company, but the troupe also had the most renowned actor of the time, Richard Burbage. Burbage was the first actor to portray Hamlet. Although Shakespeare was himself an actor, he is only known to have performed secondary roles.

Other noted actors in the troupe were William Kempe, a comedian, and Robert Asmin, a singer and dancer, both of whom were also shareholders in The King's Men. The average size for a theatrical company was twenty-five members, about half of whom would usually be shareholders. Other actors were employed part-time as needed.

Because actors in Shakespeare's time needed to project their voices for open-air performances, they tended to employ a more exaggerated, declamatory style of acting than would be acceptable to today's audiences. Some actors went to extremes, however. Shakespearean scholars generally agree that Hamlet's instruction to the Players not to "tear a passion . . . to very rags" reflects his views on the tendency to overact amongst his contemporaries. Shakespeare's presence during rehearsals of his plays would have given him the opportunity to personally instruct an actor in the way a line should be delivered.

His Verse

Although Shakespeare's dramatic output alone would have been sufficient to ensure his place among English writers, his reputation as an author does not rest solely upon his plays. He wrote poetry, as well, including the erotic narrative poems *Venus and Adonis* (1593) and *The Rape of Lucrece* (1594). He also composed 154 *Sonnets*, which were circulated in manuscript prior to their publication in 1609.

Shakespeare's poetic output was not confined to his poems, however. At the beginning of Shakespeare's career as a playwright, the prevailing style for dialog was rhyming couplets (that is, two succeeding lines of poetry that rhyme), so a high percentage of the lines in his earlier plays rhyme. In one of his early works, *Love's Labor's Lost*, for example, nearly half of the lines rhyme.

As time passed, however, Shakespeare used fewer rhymed couplets for dialog and began favoring blank verse for his plays. Blank verse consists of unrhymed lines of iambic pentameter; iambic pentameter is the technical term for lines ten syllables in length with alternating stresses (that is, an unstressed syllable followed by a stressed syllable). Although Shakespeare continued to use rhyming couplets in his plays when he wanted to indicate the end of a scene or when the situation might call for a more artificial style of speech, he favored a much more naturalistic form of expression in his later plays.

Even in his early plays, however, Shakespeare was outdoing his fellow playwrights. For example, because of the prevailing style of rhyming couplets, most of the characters in a play would sound the same; in other words, one character's "voice" could not be distinguished from that of another. In contrast, even early on Shakespeare's characters each spoke with a recognizable voice. Even without the speaker's identity being revealed, no one would have any difficulty distinguishing the innocent yet passionate utterances of Juliet from the prosaic vulgarity of her Nurse. Furthermore, if, during the course of a play, a character underwent a significant change, Shakespeare would indicate this change by altering the character's speech patterns. One example of this technique is Othello, who begins to sound more and more like Iago as he becomes progressively more infected with the "pestilence" Iago pours into his ear.

Shakespeare also used speech patterns to indicate a character's social rank. In his plays, members of the nobility usually speak in blank verse, while those of lower station speak in prose, reflecting their limited education. Shakespeare also uses prose to indicate when the more highly ranked characters are speaking informally or are under stress.

Another one of the many noteworthy aspects of Shakespeare's technique is his use of setting to reinforce ideas in his plays. In *Antony and Cleopatra*, for example, the cold austerity of Rome reflects the emotional coldness and sterility of the Romans, whereas the sun-drenched setting of Egypt reflects the passionate love of the title characters.

Furthermore, Shakespeare used imagery not only to create atmosphere but also to convey themes. *Hamlet*, for example, contains numerous references to disease and decay, reinforcing the theme of the moral and political rot in Denmark. In addition to demonstrating his technical brilliance, Shakespeare's works reveal insights into human nature that none of his predecessors or contemporaries could begin to approach.

Shakespeare's technique and contributions to drama and literature place him at the pinnacle of his art. It's no surprise then that each succeeding generation sees new additions to the ranks of "Bardolators."

As You Like It

Date

Scholars generally agree that Shakespeare wrote *As You Like It* between 1598 and 1600. It is not included in Francis Mere's list of Shakespeare's plays in *Palladis Tamia* (published in 1598); if the play were included, that would indicate that it had been written and performed by the time Mere's list was compiled. The play's entry into the Stationers' Register on August 4, 1600, demonstrates that it cannot have been written any later than that date.

Source

Thomas Lodge's *Rosalynde or Euphues' Golden Legacy* (1590) is Shakespeare's source for *As You Like It*. However, Lodge was not the originator of the story; in fact, he had borrowed it from a fourteenth century poem called "The Tale of Gamelyn." Like *As You Like It, Rosalynde* tells of the love between a young noblewoman and a younger son named Rosader who has been oppressed by his eldest brother, Saladyne. Lodge's heroine (who, like Shakespeare's, is the daughter of a banished duke whose kingdom has been usurped by another man) escapes with her friend (*not* her cousin, as in Shakespeare's version) Alinda, both of them in disguise, Rosalynde as a young man and Alinda as Aliena, his sister. Although these and other similarities are obvious, Shakespeare makes a number of significant changes. For example, he eliminates nearly all of the violence included in *Rosalynde*, and he adds several notable characters: Jaques, William, Audrey, and Touchstone. The subplot concerning Silvius and Phebe is present in both works, but whereas Lodge presents it as an idealized pastoral romance, Shakespeare highlights the shortcomings of such a relationship and uses it to demonstrate the superiority of a relationship such as that of Rosalind and Orlando.

Text

As You Like It was first published in the First Folio Edition of 1623. This text is considered by scholars to be authoritative, and all subsequent editions have been published with only minor textual differences.

As You Like It

Original Text and Modern Version

The Characters:

Duke Senior	banished duke
Duke Frederick	usurper, brother to Duke Senior
Rosalind	daughter to Duke Senior
Celia	daughter to Duke Frederick
Amiens	lord staying with the banished duke
Jaques	lord staying with the banished duke
Touchstone	court jester (or "fool")
Le Beau	courtier at Duke Frederick's court
Charles	Duke Frederick's wrestler
Oliver de Boys	eldest son of Sir Rowland de Boys
Jaques de Boys	middle son of Sir Rowland de Boys
Orlando de Boys	youngest son of Sir Rowland de Boys
Sir Oliver Martext	parish priest
Corin	shepherd
Silvius	young shepherd in love
William	country youth in love with Audrey
Audrey	goat-keeper
Phebe	shepherdess
Adam	servant to Oliver and friend to Orlando
Dennis	servant to Oliver
Hymen	god of weddings
Lords, Pages, Foresters, and Attendants	

Synopsis

Act I

Scene I   The orchard of Oliver's house
Orlando confronts Oliver about the way he has been treating him. Orlando demands his inheritance so that he can leave home and seek his fortune. Oliver plots to have Orlando killed.

Scene II   The lawn in front of the duke's palace
Rosalind and Celia try to talk Orlando out of fighting Duke Frederick's wrestler. Rosalind and Orlando fall in love at first sight.

Scene III   A room in Duke Frederick's palace
Duke Frederick accuses Rosalind of treason and banishes her. Without Duke Frederick's knowledge, Celia insists on coming with Rosalind. They decide to go disguised as brother and sister, "Ganymede" and "Aliena."

Act II

Scene I   The Forest of Arden
Duke Senior talks of the benefits of living in the forest.

Scene II   A room in Duke Frederick's palace
Duke Frederick orders a search for Celia and Rosalind.

Scene III   In front of Oliver's house
Adam warns Orlando that Oliver intends to kill him. They decide to escape together.

Scene IV   The Forest of Arden
Rosalind, Celia, and Touchstone, exhausted from their journey, meet Silvius and arrange to buy a cottage.

Act IV

    Scene I   The Forest of Arden
                    Rosalind, disguised as "Ganymede" pretending
                    to be Rosalind, teaches Orlando about love.

    Scene II   The Forest of Arden
                    Jaques and Lords celebrate the killing of a deer.

    Scene III   The Forest of Arden
                    "Ganymede" receives a love letter from Phebe.
                    Oliver comes to tell "Ganymede" and "Aliena"
                    that Orlando was injured while saving his life.

Act V

    Scene I   The Forest of Arden
                    Touchstone threatens William, telling him to give
                    up his claim to Audrey.

    Scene II   The Forest of Arden
                    Oliver confesses to Orlando that he has fallen in
                    love with "Aliena." "Ganymede" tells Orlando
                    that "he" will arrange for Orlando to marry
                    Rosalind on the following day.

    Scene III   The Forest of Arden
                    Two pages sing a love song for Audrey and
                    Touchstone.

    Scene IV   The Forest of Arden
                    Four couples are married, and Duke Senior
                    learns that his kingdom has been restored.

Epilogue   The stage
                    Rosalind bids the audience farewell.

Act one

Scene 1

Orchard of Oliver's house.

Enter **Orlando** *and* **Adam**.

Orlando   As I remember, Adam, it was upon this
fashion bequeath'd me by will but poor a thousand
crowns, and, as thou sayest, charg'd my brother,
on his blessing, to breed me well; and there begins
5   my sadness. My brother Jaques he keeps at
school, and report speaks goldenly of his profit.
For my part, he keeps me rustically at home, or (to
speak more properly) stays me here at home un-
kept; for call you that keeping for a gentleman of
10   my birth, that differs not from the stalling of an
ox? His horses are bred better, for besides that
they are fair with their feeding, they are taught
their manage, and to that end riders dearly hir'd;
but I (his brother) gain nothing under him but growth,
15   for the which his animals on his dunghills are
as much bound to him as I. Besides this nothing
that he so plentifully gives me, the something that
nature gave me his countenance seems to take from
me. He lets me feed with his hinds, bars me the
20   place of a brother, and as much as in him lies,
mines my gentility with my education. This is it,
Adam, that grieves me, and the spirit of my father,
which I think is within me, begins to mutiny against
this servitude. I will no longer endure it, though
25   yet I know no wise remedy how to avoid it.

Act one

Scene 1

The orchard of Oliver's house.

[**Orlando** *and* **Adam** *enter.*]

Orlando   [*with great frustration*] The way I remember it, Adam, my father left me an inheritance in his will of only one thousand crowns [*a crown was a coin worth about five shillings*], and, as you said, instructed my brother Oliver that, if he wished to receive his blessing, he should provide a good upbringing for me—and that was the beginning of my sadness. He pays for the university education of my brother Jaques, and his progress there is reportedly excellent. I, however, am kept home in the country, or, to be more accurate, he makes me remain here at home *without* providing for me. It isn't like you can call it "providing for" a gentleman of my social standing when it's no different from the way someone provides for an ox. His horses are better educated, for not only do they look fine from being well-fed, but they are also well-trained, and he pays a great deal to hire horse trainers. But I, his brother, have gotten nothing from him but the chance to grow up; I have as little reason to feel grateful to him as his animals living on his manure piles do. Besides this "nothing" that he gives me so much of, the things that nature did give me his lack of proper support takes away from me again. He makes me eat with his servants, refuses to treat me as a brother, and does everything he can to undermine my status as a gentleman by the way I am brought up. This, Adam, is what angers me, and my father's nature, which I think I've inherited, is beginning to rebel against being treated like a servant. I won't take it anymore, although I don't know yet any good way to change it.

Enter **Oliver**.

Adam   Yonder comes my master, your brother.

Orlando   Go apart, Adam, and thou shalt hear how
he will shake me up.

29 **Oliver**   Now, sir, what make you here?

Orlando   Nothing. I am not taught to make any thing.

Oliver   What mar you then, sir?

Orlando   Marry, sir, I am helping you to mar that
which God made, a poor unworthy brother of yours,
34 with idleness.

Oliver   Marry, sir, be better employ'd and be naught
a while.

Orlando   Shall I keep your hogs and eat husks with
them? What prodigal portion have I spent, that
I should come to such penury?

40 **Oliver**   Know you where you are, sir?

Orlando   O, sir, very well; here in your orchard.

Oliver   Know you before whom, sir?

[**Oliver** *enters.*]

Adam   Here comes my master, your brother.

Orlando   Go a little way off, Adam, and you'll hear for your-self how he bullies me.

Oliver   [*with obvious hostility*] So, sir! What are you doing here?

Orlando   [*sarcastically*] Nothing. I haven't been taught to do anything.

Oliver   Then what are you destroying, sir?

Orlando   Indeed, sir, I'm helping you destroy what God made—your poor unworthy brother—because I have nothing worthwhile to do.

Oliver   Indeed, sir, find something better to do then—go to hell!

Orlando   [*with bitter sarcasm*] Would you like me to take care of your hogs and eat their food with them? What huge inheritance have I spent that I should be reduced to such poverty? [*In Luke 15: 11–32, the prodigal son asked his father for his inheritance. After spending it all on wild living, he had to work taking care of hogs and, in order to keep from starving, he had to eat the hogs' food.*]

Oliver   Do you know where you are, sir? [*He is asking whether* **Orlando** *knows whom he is daring to speak so disrespectfully to.*]

Orlando   [*deliberately misunderstanding* **Oliver**, *taking his question literally to annoy him*] Oh, yes, sir, very well. I'm here in your garden.

Oliver   Do you know whom you are talking to?

Orlando   Ay, better than him I am before knows me.
I know you are my eldest brother, and in the gentle
45   condition of blood you should so know me.
The courtesy of nations allows you my better, in
that you are the first born, but the same tradition
takes not away my blood, were there twenty brothers
betwixt us. I have as much of my father in me
as you, albeit I confess your coming before me is
51   nearer to his reverence.

Oliver   What, boy!

[Strikes him.]

Orlando   Come, come, elder brother, you are too
young in this.

[Collaring him.]

55 **Oliver**   Wilt thou lay hands on me, villain?

Orlando   I am no villain; I am the youngest son of
Sir Rowland de Boys. He was my father, and he
is thrice a villain that says such a father begot
villains. Wert thou not my brother, I would not
take this hand from thy throat till this other had
pull'd out thy tongue for saying so. Thou hast
62   rail'd on thyself.

Adam   Sweet masters, be patient, for your
father's remembrance, be at accord.

65 **Oliver**   Let me go, I say.

Orlando   Yes, better than the one I'm talking to knows me. I know you are my eldest brother, and you should acknowledge that I am as much a gentleman as you are. The accepted custom of the time says that you are superior to me since you are the first-born, but that same tradition doesn't take away my family ancestry, even if there were twenty brothers between us in age. I have as much of my father in me as you, although I admit that your being older than I gives you a strong claim to the respect which was his. [*The "custom of the time" refers to the custom of primogeniture in which the eldest son would inherit his father's entire estate.*]

Oliver   Take that, boy! [**Oliver** *slaps* **Orlando** *across the face.*]

Orlando   [*grabbing* **Oliver** *by the throat*] Come, come, older brother, you're a very inexperienced fighter!

Oliver   [*struggling to break free*] Do you dare to touch me, villain?

Orlando   [*taking the word "villain" in its other sense*] I'm not a peasant; I'm the youngest son of Sir Rowland de Boys. He was my father, and anyone who says that a man like him fathered peasants is a far worse villain! If you weren't my brother, I wouldn't let go of your throat until I'd pulled out your tongue for saying so. You have insulted yourself.

Adam   [*hurrying forward to stop the fight*] Dear masters, calm down! For the sake of your father's memory, stop fighting!

Oliver   [*through gritted teeth*] Let me go, I tell you!

Orlando   I will not till I please. You shall hear me.
My father charg'd you in his will to give me good
education. You have train'd me like a peasant,
obscuring and hiding from me all gentleman-like
70   qualities. The spirit of my father grows strong
in me, and I will no longer endure it; therefore
allow me such exercises as may become a gentleman,
73   or give me the poor allottery my father left me
by testament, with that I will go buy my fortunes.

Oliver   And what wilt thou do? beg, when that is
spent? Well, sir, get you in. I will not long be
troubled with you; you shall have some part of
your will. I pray you leave me.

Orlando   I will no further offend you than becomes
80   me for my good.

Oliver   Get you with him, you old dog.

Adam   Is "old dog" my reward? Most true, I
have lost my teeth in your service. God be with my
84   old master, he would not have spoke such a word.

Exeunt **Orlando**, **Adam**.

Oliver   Is it even so? Begin you to grow upon me?
I will physic your rankness, and yet give no thousand crowns neither. Holla, Dennis!

Enter **Dennis**.

Dennis   Calls your worship?

Oliver   Was not Charles, the Duke's wrastler, here
90   to speak with me?

Orlando   I won't until I'm ready! You're going to listen to me. In his will my father instructed you to give me a good education. You've raised me like a peasant, obscuring and hiding all the gentlemanly accomplishments. My father's nature is growing strong in me, and I won't put up with your treatment of me any longer. Therefore, provide the training for me that I should have as a gentleman or give me the small inheritance my father left me in his will; with it I will go seek my fortune.

Oliver   [*sneeringly*] And what will you do when you've spent it all? Beg? Well, sir, go inside. I won't be annoyed by you much longer. You shall have at least part of what you want. Please just go away.

Orlando   I won't be here to bother you any more than I can help being.

Oliver   [*coldly, to* **Adam**] You go with him, you old dog.

Adam   [*deeply hurt and offended*] Is being called an "old dog" my reward? It's true; I'm so old that I've lost all my teeth from age while I have been your servant. God bless my old master! He wouldn't have said such a thing to me.

[**Orlando** *and* **Adam** *leave.*]

Oliver   [*to the now-absent* **Orlando**] Is that how it is? Do you think you can get out of hand? I'll give you a dose of medicine that will cure your impudence, and I won't have to give a thousand crowns to do it.

[*calling for his servant*] Hey, Dennis!

[**Dennis** *enters.*]

Dennis   Did you call, Your Worship?

Oliver   Wasn't Charles, the duke's wrestler, here to speak to me?

Dennis   So please you, he is here at the door, and importunes access to you.

Oliver   Call him in. [*Exit* **Dennis**.] 'Twill be a good way; and to-morrow the wrastling is.

Enter **Charles**.

95 **Charles**   Good morrow to your worship.

Oliver   Good Monsieur Charles, what's the new news at the new court?

Charles   There's no news at the court, sir, but the old news: that is, the old Duke is banish'd by his
100   younger brother the new Duke, and three or four loving lords have put themselves into voluntary exile with him, whose lands and revenues enrich the new Duke; therefore he gives them good leave to wander.

Oliver   Can you tell if Rosalind, the Duke's daugh-
106   ter, be banish'd with her father?

Charles   O no; for the Duke's daughter, her cousin, so loves her, being ever from their cradles bred together, that [she] would have follow'd her exile, or
110   have died to stay behind her. She is at the court, and no less belov'd of her uncle than his own daughter, and never two ladies lov'd as they do.

Oliver   Where will the old Duke live?

Dennis   Yes, he is here at the door, asking to see you.

Oliver   Call him in.

[**Dennis** *bows and exits.*]

[*to himself*] It will be a good way to handle this, and tomorrow is the wrestling match.

[**Charles** *enters.*]

Charles   Good morning to you, Your Worship.

Oliver   Good Mister Charles, what new news is there at the new court?

Charles   There's no news at the court, sir, but the old news: that is, the old duke has been banished by his younger brother, the new duke, and three or four loyal lords have, of their own free will, gone into exile with him. The new duke is getting rich off their lands and incomes, so he has gladly allowed them to go.

Oliver   Do you know if Rosalind, the duke's daughter, has been banished with her father?

Charles   Oh, no, for the duke's daughter Celia, her cousin, loves her so much, having been raised with her from the time they were infants, that she would have followed Rosalind into exile or died of grief had she stayed behind. Rosalind is at the court and is loved by her uncle, Duke Frederick, as much as his own daughter. There have never been two ladies who have loved one another as they do.

Oliver   Where does the old duke live?

Charles   They say he is already in the forest of Arden,
115   and a many merry men with him; and there
they live like the old Robin Hood of England. They
say many young gentlemen flock to him every day,
and fleet the time carelessly, as they did in the golden
world.

Oliver   What, you wrastle to-morrow before the
121   new Duke?

Charles   Marry, do I, sir; and I came to acquaint
you with a matter. I am given, sir, secretly to
124   understand that your younger brother, Orlando,
hath a disposition to come in disguis'd against me
to try a fall. To-morrow, sir, I wrastle for my
credit, and he that escapes me without some broken
limb shall acquit him well. Your brother is but
129   young and tender, and for your love I would
be loath to foil him, as I must for my own honor
if he come in; therefore out of my love to you,
I came hither to acquaint you withal, that either
you might stay him from his intendment, or brook
134   such disgrace well as he shall run into, in that it
is a thing of his own search, and altogether against
my will.

Charles   They say he is already in the Forest of Arden, and many merry men are with him; there they live like the old Robin Hood of England and his men. They say that many young gentlemen join Duke Senior every day and pass the time without any worries, as they did in the Golden Age. [*In Greek mythology, the Golden Age was an idyllic time in the distant past when humans lived without working on the bounty of nature in a continual springtime.*]

Oliver   So, are you wrestling tomorrow for the new duke?

Charles   Indeed, I am, sir, and I came to tell you about something. I have been told secretly, sir, that your younger brother Orlando is intending to come in disguise to wrestle with me. Tomorrow, sir, I will wrestle so as to uphold my reputation, and he who gets away without a broken bone will have to show that he's an excellent wrestler. Your brother is young and inexperienced, and for your sake I would hate to defeat him, as I must for my honor's sake if he challenges me. Therefore, because of my loyalty to you, I came here to tell you about it, so that you may either keep him from doing as he plans or endure the disgrace that he'll cause, which will be his own fault and not at all what I want.

Oliver   Charles, I thank thee for thy love to me,
which thou shalt find I will most kindly requite.
139   I had myself notice of my brother's purpose
herein, and have by underhand means labor'd to
dissuade him from it; but he is resolute. I'll tell
thee, Charles, it is the stubbornest young fellow of
France, full of ambition, an envious emulator of
144   every man's good parts, a secret and villainous
contriver against me his natural brother; therefore
use thy discretion—I had as lief thou didst break
his neck as his finger. And thou wert best look
to't; for if thou dost him any slight disgrace, or if
149   he do not mightily grace himself on thee, he
will practice against thee by poison, entrap thee by
some treacherous device, and never leave thee till
he hath ta'en thy life by some indirect means or
other; for I assure thee (and almost with tears I
154   speak it) there is not one so young and so villainous this day living. I speak but brotherly of
him, but should I anatomize him to thee as he is, I
must blush and weep, and thou must look pale and
wonder.

Charles   I am heartily glad I came hither to you.
160   If he come to-morrow, I'll give him his payment.
If ever he go alone again, I'll never wrastle for prize
more. And so God keep your worship!

Exit.

Oliver [*with false earnestness*] I thank you for your loyalty
to me, Charles, which you'll see that I will generously
repay. I, too, was told about my brother's intention, and I've
tried, without letting him know about it, to get him to give
up the idea, but he's determined. I tell you, Charles, he is
the most ruthless young fellow in France. He's full of ambition, he maliciously criticizes every other man's good qualities, and he's a sneaky and villainous schemer against me,
his own brother. So do as you wish to him. I would just as
soon have you break his neck as his finger. And you had
better beware, for if you embarrass him even a little or if he
doesn't greatly increase his reputation at your expense, he
will plot against you to poison you or to trap you by some
devious scheme, and he won't leave you alone until he has
killed you, one underhanded way or another. For, I assure
you—and it almost makes me weep to say it—there is no
one alive today who is so young and yet so wicked as he is.
Even though I'm his brother, I'm saying these things, but if I
were to tell you all his faults, I would have to blush and
weep from shame, and you would turn white with shock.

Charles I'm very glad I came to see you. If he comes tomorrow, I'll give him what's coming to him. If he can ever walk
without help again, I'll never wrestle for money anymore.
And so goodbye, Your Worship!

Oliver   Farewell, good Charles. Now will I
164   stir this gamester. I hope I shall see an end
of him; for my soul (yet I know not why) hates
nothing more than he. Yet he's gentle, never school'd
and yet learned, full of noble device, of all sorts
enchantingly belov'd, and indeed so much in the
169   heart of the world, and especially of my own
people, who best know him, that I am altogether
mispris'd. But it shall not be so long, this wrastler
shall clear all. Nothing remains but that I kindle
the boy thither, which now I'll go about.

Exit.

Scene 2

Enter **Rosalind** *and* **Celia**.

Celia   I pray thee, Rosalind, sweet my coz, be
merry.

Rosalind   Dear Celia—I show more mirth than I am
mistress of, and would you yet [I] were merrier?
5   Unless you could teach me to forget a banish'd
father, you must not learn me how to remember
any extraordinary pleasure.

Oliver   Farewell, Charles.

[**Charles** *leaves, shaking his head.*]

[*to himself, speaking of* **Orlando**] Now I'll goad this
"athlete" to compete. I hope it's the death of him, for
although I don't know why, I hate him more than anything
in the world, to the depths of my soul. He acts like a gentleman, he's intelligent even though he's never had proper
schooling, and his attitudes are noble. He's loved by all
kinds of people, almost as if he had cast a spell on them,
and in fact he's so much adored by the world, and especially my own servants, who know him best, that everyone
completely despises me. But it won't be like this for long.
This wrestler will take care of everything. All I have to do is
incite the boy to wrestle, which I'll go do now.

[**Oliver** *leaves.*]

Scene 2

The lawn in front of the duke's palace.

[**Celia** *and* **Rosalind** *enter.*]

Celia   [*coaxingly*] Please, Rosalind, my sweet cousin, be
happy.

Rosalind   [*sighing*] Dear Celia, I'm already trying to appear
more cheerful than I am, yet you want me to be even
happier? Unless you can teach me how to forget a banished
father, you mustn't instruct me to remember any great
happiness.

Celia   Herein I see thou lov'st me not with the full
weight that I love thee. If my uncle, thy banish'd
10   father, had banished thy uncle, the Duke my
father, so thou hadst been still with me, I could
have taught my love to take thy father for mine;
so wouldst thou, if the truth of thy love to me were
14   so righteously temper'd as mine is to thee.

Rosalind   Well, I will forget the condition of my estate,
to rejoice in yours.

Celia   You know my father hath no child but I,
nor none is like to have; and truly when he dies,
19   thou shalt be his heir; for what he hath taken
away from thy father perforce, I will render thee
again in affection. By mine honor, I will, and when
I break that oath, let me turn monster. Therefore,
my sweet Rose, my dear Rose, be merry.

Rosalind   From henceforth I will, coz, and devise
sports. Let me see—what think you of falling in love?

Celia   Marry, I prithee do, to make sport withal.
27   But love no man in good earnest, nor no further
in sport neither, than with safety of a pure blush
thou mayst in honor come off again.

Rosalind   What shall be our sport then?

Celia [*with gentle reproach*] I see from this that you don't love me as much as I love you. If Duke Senior, your banished father, had banished my father, Duke Frederick, as long as you were still with me, I could have taught myself to love your father as if he were mine. That's what you would do if your love for me were truly as strong as mine is for you.

Rosalind [*forcing a smile*] Well, I will forget about my situation in order to be happy about yours.

Celia You know that I am my father's only child, and he is unlikely to have any more. I promise you that when he dies you shall be his heir. Because of my affection for you, I will give back to you what he has taken away from your father by force. I swear that I will, and if I break my vow may I turn into a monster. Therefore, my sweet Rose, my dear Rose, be happy.

Rosalind From now on I will, cousin, and I'll think up fun things to do. Let me see. What do you think of falling in love?

Celia By all means, do so, but only to have fun. But don't truly love a man or even go beyond a flirtation that you can safely escape with only an innocent blush, and so keep your honor.

Rosalind What shall we do to amuse ourselves, then?

31 **Celia**   Let us sit and mock the good huswife
Fortune from her wheel, that her gifts may henceforth be bestow'd equally.

Rosalind   I would we could do so; for her benefits
are mightily misplac'd, and the bountiful blind
36   woman doth most mistake in her gifts to women.

Celia   'Tis true, for those that she makes fair she
scarce makes honest, and those that she makes honest
she makes very ill-favoredly.

Rosalind   Nay, now thou goest from Fortune's office
to Nature's. Fortune reigns in gifts of the world,
42   not in the lineaments of Nature.

Enter Clown [**Touchstone**].

Celia   No; when Nature hath made a fair crea-
ture, may she not by Fortune fall into the fire?
45   Though Nature hath given us wit to flout at
Fortune, hath not Fortune sent in this fool to cut off
the argument?

Celia   Let's sit and tease Fortune, the good "housewife," to leave her spinning wheel, so that from now on she will give her gifts away equally. [*People thought of Fortune as being like a goddess who had a wheel that determined the good or bad things that happened to them.* **Celia** *puns that Fortune's wheel is a spinning wheel like that used by housewives, but she pronounces the word "housewife" as "hussif" in order to jokingly imply that Fortune is as untrustworthy as a hussy (that is, a whore).*]

Rosalind   I wish we could do so, for her gifts are definitely given to the wrong people, and generous blind woman that she is, she is most wrong in her gifts to women. [*Fortune was often depicted as being blind to indicate her impartiality.*]

Celia   That's true, for the ones she gives beauty to aren't sexually pure as a rule, and those she gives purity to she also makes very homely.

Rosalind   [*shaking her head and laughing*] No, now you're talking about what Nature does, not Fortune. Fortune is in charge of worldly gifts, not how a person looks; that comes from Nature. [*At that time, people believed that things like wealth and power were given by Fortune, as opposed to beauty and intelligence, which were believed to come from Nature.*]

Celia   Oh, no? When Nature has created a beautiful woman, can't Fortune make her fall into the fire?

[**Touchstone** *enters.*]

Although Nature has given us the intelligence to make fun of Fortune, hasn't Fortune sent this fool to stop our debate? [**Touchstone** *was the court jester, also called the court's "fool."*]

Rosalind   Indeed, there is Fortune too hard for Nature,
when Fortune makes Nature's natural the cutter-off
50   of Nature's wit.

Celia   Peradventure this is not Fortune's work
neither, but Nature's, who perceiveth our natural
wits too dull to reason of such goddesses, [and] hath
sent this natural for our whetstone; for always the
55   dullness of the fool is the whetstone of the wits.
How now, wit, whither wander you?

Touchstone   Mistress, you must come away to your
father.

Celia   Were you made the messenger?

Touchstone   No, by mine honor, but I was bid to
61   come for you.

Rosalind   Where learn'd you that oath, fool?

Touchstone   Of a certain knight, that swore by his
honor they were good pancakes, and swore by his
honor the mustard was naught. Now I'll stand to it,
the pancakes were naught, and the mustard was good,
67   and yet was not the knight forsworn.

Celia   How prove you that, in the great heap of
your knowledge?

Rosalind   Ay, marry, now unmuzzle your wisdom.

Touchstone   Stand you both forth now. Stroke your
72   chins, and swear by your beards that I am a
knave.

Celia   By our beards (if we had them) thou art.

Rosalind   Indeed, in that case Fortune wins out over Nature, when Fortune can make Nature's natural fool the one who cuts off Nature's gift of intelligence.

Celia   Perhaps this isn't Fortune's doing either but rather Nature's, who sees that our natural intelligence isn't sharp enough to understand goddesses like them and has sent this fool to be our whetstone. The mental dullness of fools is always the whetstone for sharpening wits. [*Whetstones were used to sharpen knives.*]

[*to* **Touchstone**] Hello there, wit! Where are you wandering to?

Touchstone   [*bowing formally*] Mistress, you must go see your father.

Celia   Are you the messenger?

Touchstone   No, I swear on my honor, but I was told to come for you.

Rosalind   Where did you learn to say, "On my honor," fool?

Touchstone   From a certain knight who swore by *his* honor that the pancakes were good and swore by his honor that the mustard was bad, but I'll swear to it that the pancakes were bad and the mustard was good. And yet the knight wasn't lying.

Celia   How will you prove that, out of the great heap of your knowledge?

Rosalind   Yes, indeed, now unmuzzle your wisdom.

Touchstone   Pay attention now. Stroke your chins and swear by your beards that I am a dishonest fellow.

Celia   [*stroking her chin and chuckling*] We swear by our beards (if we had them) that you are.

Touchstone   By my knavery (if I had it) then I were.
76   But if you swear by that that is not, you are not
forsworn. No more was this knight, swearing by
his honor, for he never had any; or if he had, he
had sworn it away before ever he saw those pancakes
80   or that mustard.

Celia   Prithee, who is't that thou mean'st?

Touchstone   One that old Frederick, your father, loves.

Celia   My father's love is enough to honor him
enough. Speak no more of him, you'll be whipt for
85   taxation one of these days.

Touchstone   The more pity that fools may not speak
wisely what wise men do foolishly.

Celia   By my troth, thou sayest true; for since the
89   little wit that fools have was silenc'd, the little
foolery that wise men have makes a great show.
Here comes Monsieur [Le] Beau.

Enter **Le Beau**.

Rosalind   With his mouth full of news.

Celia   Which he will put on us, as pigeons feed
their young.

95 **Rosalind**   Then shall we be news-cramm'd.

Celia   All the better; we shall be the more market-
able. *Bon jour*, Monsieur Le Beau. What's the
news?

Touchstone   By my dishonesty (if I had it), I *would* be a dishonest fellow. But if you swear by something that doesn't exist, you're not lying. So then the knight wasn't really swearing by his honor because he never had any. Or if he had, he had sworn it away long before he saw those pancakes or that mustard.

Celia   [*very much intrigued*] Tell me, who are you talking about?

Touchstone   Someone old Frederick, your father, loves.

Celia   [*defensively*] My father's love is a good enough reason to respect him. That's enough! Don't say anything more about him, or you'll be whipped for slander one of these days.

Touchstone   [*shaking his head regretfully*] It's a great shame that fools aren't allowed to speak wisely about the foolish things that wise men do.

Celia   [*sighing regretfully*] Indeed, you're telling the truth, for ever since the little wit that fools like you have was silenced, the little foolishness of wise men has been all too obvious. Here comes Le Beau.

[**Le Beau** *enters.*]

Rosalind   With his mouth full of news.

Celia   [*with twinkling eyes*] Which he'll force-feed us, the way pigeons feed their young.

Rosalind   Then we shall be crammed with news.

Celia   [*jokingly*] That's good! Then we'll be more easily sold at market. [*In order to bring a better price, pigeons and other edible birds were fattened up before being sold.*]

Good day, Monsieur Le Beau. What's the news?
[*"Monsieur" is French for "mister."*]

Le Beau   Fair princess, you have lost much good
100   sport.

Celia   Sport! of what color?

Le Beau   What color, madam? How shall I answer you?

Rosalind   As wit and fortune will.

105 **Touchstone**   Or as the Destinies decrees.

Celia   Well said—that was laid on with a trowel.

Touchstone   Nay, if I keep not my rank—

Rosalind   Thou losest thy old smell.

Le Beau   You amaze me, ladies. I would have
told you of good wrastling, which you have lost
111   the sight of.

Rosalind   Yet tell us the manner of the wrastling.

Le Beau   I will tell you the beginning; and if it
114   please your ladyships, you may see the end, for
the best is yet to do, and here where you are, they
are coming to perform it.

Celia   Well, the beginning, that is dead and buried.

Le Beau   There comes an old man and his three
sons—

Celia   I could match this beginning with an old tale.

Le Beau   Lovely princess, you've missed some excellent sport.

Celia   Sport? Of what kind?

Le Beau   What kind, madam! I don't know how to answer you.

Rosalind   However your cleverness and good luck will allow.

Touchstone   Or as the Destinies command. [*The Destinies (or Fates), in Greek mythology, were believed to control what happened to all individuals from the time they were born to the time they died.*]

Celia   A very good reply! You laid it on thick.

Touchstone   No, if I don't maintain my rank—

Rosalind   [**Touchstone** *means that he needs to uphold his reputation as jester, but* **Rosalind** *interrupts him, punning on the word "rank."*] You'll lose your old body odor.

Le Beau   [*shaking his head at the ladies' wordplay*] You confuse me, ladies. I intended to tell you about some good wrestling, which you've missed seeing.

Rosalind   Tell us how the wrestling went.

Le Beau   I'll tell you how it began, and if you wish, your ladyships, you may watch the end because the best is yet to happen, and they are coming here, where you are, to perform it.

Celia   Well, tell the beginning, which is dead and buried.

Le Beau   An old man and his three sons came along—

Celia   I could tell the end of an old fairy tale that begins like this.

Le Beau   Three proper young men, of excellent
122   growth and presence.

Rosalind   With bills on their necks, "Be it known unto
all men by these presents."

Le Beau   The eldest of the three wrastled with
Charles, the Duke's wrastler, which Charles in a
127   moment threw him, and broke three of his ribs,
that there is little hope of life in him. So he serv'd
the second, and so the third. Yonder they lie, the
poor old man, their father, making such pitiful dole
over them that all the beholders take his part with
132   weeping.

Rosalind   Alas!

Touchstone   But what is the sport, monsieur, that the
135   ladies have lost?

Le Beau   Why, this that I speak of.

Touchstone   Thus men may grow wiser every day.
It is the first time that ever I heard breaking of ribs
was sport for ladies.

140 **Celia**   Or I, I promise thee.

Rosalind   But is there any else longs to see this broken
music in his sides? Is there yet another dotes upon
rib-breaking? Shall we see this wrastling, cousin?

Le Beau   [*with dignity, ignoring the interruption*] Three well-built young men, very tall and having an impressive sort of presence—

Rosalind   With signs hanging from their necks reading: "Let all men know by these presents—" [*She puns, referring to a phrase which appeared at the beginning of legal documents: "Be it known unto all men by this present document."*]

Le Beau   [*with dogged persistence*] The eldest of the three wrestled with Charles, the duke's wrestler. In an instant, Charles threw him and broke three of his ribs. There's little hope he'll survive. Charles did the same to the second and then the third. They lie over there. The poor old man, their father, is weeping so pitifully over them that all the onlookers join him in crying.

Rosalind   How sad!

Touchstone   But what is the entertainment, sir, that the ladies have missed?

Le Beau   Why, that which I just told you about.

Touchstone   [*shaking his head in mock admiration*] This is how people grow wiser every day! It's the first time I've ever heard that breaking ribs was appropriate entertainment for ladies.

Celia   I certainly haven't either.

Rosalind   But does anyone else want to see this "music" of breaking ribs? Does anyone else enjoy rib-breaking? Shall we watch this wrestling, cousin? [**Rosalind** *is punning; "broken music" refers to music written in parts for different instruments.*]

Le Beau   You must, if you stay here, for here is
the place appointed for the wrastling, and they are
146   ready to perform it.

Celia   Yonder sure they are coming. Let us now
stay and see it.

Flourish. Enter **Duke [Frederick]**, **Lords**, **Orlando**,
Charles, *and* **Attendants**.

Duke Frederick   Come on. Since the youth will not be
150   entreated, his own peril on his forwardness.

Rosalind   Is yonder the man?

Le Beau   Even he, madam.

Celia   Alas, he is too young! yet he looks success-
fully.

Duke Frederick   How now, daughter and cousin? are you
156   crept hither to see the wrastling?

Rosalind   Ay, my liege, so please you give us leave.

Duke Frederick   You will take little delight in it, I can
tell you, there is such odds in the man. In pity of
160   the challenger's youth I would fain dissuade
him, but he will not be entreated. Speak to him,
ladies, see if you can move him.

Celia   Call him hither, good Monsieur Le Beau.

Duke Frederick   Do so; I'll not be by.

Le Beau   Monsieur the challenger, the princesses
166   call for you.

Orlando   I attend them with all respect and duty.

Le Beau   You'll have to, if you stay here; this is where the wrestling is to be held, and they are ready to perform it.

Celia   Yes, here they come. Let's stay now and see it.

[*Trumpets sound.* **Duke Frederick**, **Lords**, **Orlando**, **Charles**, *and* **Attendants** *enter.*]

Duke Frederick   Come on. Since this young man won't be talked out of it, he's responsible for his own recklessness.

Rosalind   [*clearly impressed by* **Orlando's** *appearance*] Is that the man there?

Le Beau   That's the one, madam.

Celia   Oh dear, he's too young! Although he does look as if he could succeed.

Duke Frederick   Hello, daughter and niece! Have you snuck here to see the wrestling?

Rosalind   Yes, My Lord, if you will allow us to do so.

Duke Frederick   You won't enjoy it much, I warn you. The odds are very much in Charles' favor. Feeling sorry for the challenger because of his youth, I did my best to talk him out of it, but he won't listen. Talk to him, ladies; see if you can persuade him.

Celia   Call him here, dear Monsieur Le Beau.

Duke Frederick   Yes, do. I'll move away from here. [*He steps away from the group.*]

Le Beau   [*calling out to* **Orlando**] Monsieur Challenger, the princesses want to talk to you.

Orlando   I'll come to them with all respect and duty. [*He walks over to* **Celia** *and* **Rosalind** *and bows.*]

Rosalind   Young man, have you challeng'd Charles
the wrastler?

Orlando   No, fair princess; he is the general challenger. I come but in, as others do, to try with him
172   the strength of my youth.

Celia   Young gentleman, your spirits are too bold
for your years. You have seen cruel proof of this
man's strength. If you saw yourself with your eyes,
176   or knew yourself with your judgment, the
fear of your adventure would counsel you to a more
equal enterprise. We pray you for your own sake
to embrace your own safety, and give over this attempt.

180 **Rosalind**   Do, young sir, your reputation shall
not therefore be mispris'd. We will make it our suit
to the Duke that the wrastling might not go forward.

Orlando   I beseech you, punish me not with your hard
thoughts, wherein I confess me much guilty to deny
so fair and excellent ladies any thing. But let your
186   fair eyes and gentle wishes go with me to my
trial; wherein if I be foil'd, there is but one sham'd
that was never gracious; if kill'd, but one dead that
is willing to be so. I shall do my friends no wrong,
for I have none to lament me; the world no injury,
for in it I have nothing. Only in the world I fill up a
place, which may be better supplied when I have
193   made it empty.

Rosalind   The little strength that I have, I would it
were with you.

Celia   And mine, to eke out hers.

Rosalind   Fare you well; pray heaven I be deceiv'd
198   in you!

Rosalind   Young man, have you challenged Charles, the wrestler?

Orlando   No, lovely princess. He has issued a general challenge. I've merely come, as the others have, to test him with my youthful strength.

Celia   Young gentleman, your courage is greater than your age. You have seen the cruel evidence of this man's strength. If you could really see yourself or use your judgment to know yourself, fear of what you're about to do would tell you to undertake a challenge more suited to your ability. We urge you, for your own sake, to think of your own safety and not attempt to do this thing.

Rosalind   Please do, young sir. Your reputation will not be harmed because of it. We will ask Duke Frederick to call off the wrestling match.

Orlando   I beg you not to think badly of me if I refuse to withdraw. I confess that I feel guilty to deny such lovely and excellent ladies anything. But let your beautiful eyes and good wishes support me in my test. If I am defeated, I'm the only one to be shamed, and no one has ever thought well of me anyway. If I am killed, I'm willing to die. I will be doing my friends no harm, for I have none to mourn me. I won't be harming the world, for I have nothing in it; I merely take up space in the world, which may be filled better by someone else when I have left it empty.

Rosalind   [*unable to keep from staring at* **Orlando**] I wish I could give you the little strength I have.

Celia   And mine, to add to hers.

Rosalind   Good luck. I pray to heaven that I'm wrong about your chances.

Celia   Your heart's desires be with you!

Charles   Come, where is this young gallant that is so
201   desirous to lie with his mother earth?

Orlando   Ready, sir, but his will hath in it a more
modest working.

Duke Frederick   You shall try but one fall.

Charles   No, I warrant your Grace, you shall not
entreat him to a second, that have so mightily per-
207   suaded him from a first.

Orlando   You mean to mock me after; you should not
have mock'd me before. But come your ways.

Rosalind   Now Hercules be thy speed, young man!

Celia   I would I were invisible, to catch the strong
212   fellow by the leg.

Wrastle.

Rosalind   O excellent young man!

Celia   If I had a thunderbolt in mine eye, I can tell
who should down.

[**Charles** *is thrown.*] *Shout.*

216 **Duke Frederick**   No more, no more.

Orlando   Yes, I beseech your Grace, I am not yet
well breath'd.

Celia   May you get your heart's desires!

Charles   [*striding in*] Come, where is the young fellow who is so eager to lie with mother earth?

Orlando   [*Catching* **Charles'** *double entendre,* **Orlando** *takes the word "lie" in a sexual sense instead of as a reference to dying.*] Ready, sir, but I have a more modest job in mind.

Duke Frederick   [*moving to rejoin the group*] You shall have only one fall.

Charles   No, I assure you, Your Grace, you won't be able to talk him into trying again any more than you could talk him out of the first fall.

Orlando   Don't celebrate your victory before you have even won it. Now, come on.

Rosalind   [*calling out*] May Hercules give you success, young man! [*Hercules was a mythological hero noted for his great strength.*]

Celia   I wish I could make myself invisible so that I could grab Charles' leg.

[**Charles** and **Orlando** *wrestle.*]

Rosalind   [*excitedly*] Oh, what an excellent young man!

Celia   If I could shoot thunderbolts from my eyes, I know who would go down.

[**Orlando** *throws* **Charles** *down. The watching crowd cheers.*]

Duke Frederick   Stop the match! Stop the match!

Orlando   [*panting from his exertions*] Yes, let us continue, Your Grace. I'm hardly even warmed up.

Duke Frederick   How dost thou, Charles?

220 **Le Beau**   He cannot speak, my lord.

Duke Frederick   Bear him away. What is thy name,
young man?

Orlando   Orlando, my liege, the youngest son of Sir
Rowland de Boys.

Duke Frederick   I would thou hadst been son to some
man else:
225 The world esteem'd thy father honorable,
But I did find him still mine enemy.
Thou shouldst have better pleas'd me with this deed
Hadst thou descended from another house.
But fare thee well, thou art a gallant youth.
230 I would thou hadst told me of another father.

Exit **Duke** [*with* **Train** *and* **Le Beau**].

Celia   Were I my father, coz, would I do this?

Orlando   I am more proud to be Sir Rowland's son,
His youngest son, and would not change that calling
To be adopted heir to Frederick.

235 **Rosalind**   My father lov'd Sir Rowland as his soul,
And all the world was of my father's mind.
Had I before known this young man his son,
I should have given him tears unto entreaties,
Ere he should thus have ventur'd.

Duke Frederick   How are you, Charles?

Le Beau   He can't speak, My Lord.

Duke Frederick   Carry him away. [**Attendants** *carry* **Charles** *out.*]

[*kindly, to* **Orlando**] What is your name, young man?

Orlando   [*bowing formally*] Orlando, My Lord, the youngest son of Sir Rowland de Boys.

Duke Frederick   [*stiffening upon hearing the name of* **Orlando's** *father*] I would have preferred that you had been someone else's son. The whole world thought your father was an honorable man, yet I considered him to be my enemy nonetheless. You would have pleased me better with what you have done if you had come from another family. But good luck to you. You are a brave young man. [*He shakes his head regretfully.*] I wish you had had a different father.

[**Duke Frederick**, **Le Beau**, **Lords**, *and* **Attendants** *leave.*]

Celia   [*to* **Rosalind**, *looking after her departing father with a troubled expression*] If I were my father, cousin, would I act like this?

Orlando   I am very proud to be Sir Rowland's son—his youngest son—and I wouldn't change who I am, not even to be Duke Frederick's adopted heir.

Rosalind   [*to* **Celia**] My father loved Sir Rowland as much as he loved his own soul, and all the rest of the world had the same opinion of him as my father had. If I had known before that this young man was his son, I would have added tears to my pleas before he had made such an attempt.

Celia   Gentle cousin,
240   Let us go thank him, and encourage him.
       My father's rough and envious disposition
       Sticks me at heart. Sir, you have well deserv'd.
       If you do keep your promises in love
       But justly as you have exceeded all promise,
       Your mistress shall be happy.

245 **Rosalind**   Gentleman,

                    [*Giving him a chain from her neck.*]

     Wear this for me: one out of suits with Fortune,
     That could give more, but that her hand lacks means.

     Shall we go, coz?

     Celia   Ay. Fare you well, fair gentleman.

     Orlando   Can I not say, I thank you? My better
           parts
           Are all thrown down, and that which here stands up
251   Is but a quintain, a mere liveless block.

     Rosalind   He calls us back. My pride fell with my
           fortunes,
           I'll ask him what he would. Did you call, sir?
           Sir, you have wrastled well, and overthrown
           More than your enemies.

255 **Celia**   Will you go, coz?

     Rosalind   Have with you.—Fare you well.

                    Exit [*with* **Celia**].

60

Celia   Dear Cousin, let's go thank him and encourage him.

[*to herself*] My father's rough and spiteful behavior stabs me to the heart.

[*to* **Orlando**] Sir, you truly deserve your triumph. If you keep your vows of love as well as you have kept your promise to win, going beyond what anyone expected, your wife will be very fortunate.

Rosalind   Sir [*she pauses to give him a chain from around her neck*], wear this for me, a person not in favor with Fortune. I would give you more, but I'm not able to do so.

[*to* **Celia**] Shall we go, Cousin?

Celia   Yes.

[*to* **Orlando**] Good luck to you, good sir. [*She and* **Rosalind** *begin to walk away.*]

Orlando   [*to himself*] Can't I even say, "Thank you"? My intelligence has been tossed to the mat, and what is standing here is just a lifeless wooden jousting dummy.

Rosalind   [*whispering excitedly, to* **Celia**] He is calling us back!

[*to herself*] I lost my pride when I lost my good fortune. I'll ask him what he wants.

[*to* **Orlando**] Did you call, sir? Sir, you have wrestled well and conquered more than just your enemies. [*She means that she has been "conquered," that is, that she has fallen in love with him.* **Rosalind** *and* **Orlando** *gaze into one another's eyes.*]

Celia   Are you coming, Cousin?

Rosalind   Yes, I'm coming with you.

[*to* **Orlando**] Goodbye.

[**Rosalind** *and* **Celia** *leave as* **Orlando** *watches silently.*]

61

Orlando   What passion hangs these weights upon my
tongue?
I cannot speak to her, yet she urg'd conference.

Enter **Le Beau**.

O poor Orlando! thou art overthrown,
260   Or Charles, or something weaker, masters thee.

Le Beau   Good sir, I do in friendship counsel you
To leave this place. Albeit you have deserv'd
High commendation, true applause, and love,
Yet such is now the Duke's condition
265   That he misconsters all that you have done.
The Duke is humorous—what he is indeed
More suits you to conceive than I to speak of.

Orlando   I thank you, sir; and pray you tell me this:
Which of the two was daughter of the Duke,
270   That here was at the wrastling?

Le Beau   Neither his daughter, if we judge by
manners,
But yet indeed the [smaller] is his daughter.
The other is daughter to the banish'd Duke,
And here detain'd by her usurping uncle
275   To keep his daughter company, whose loves
Are dearer than the natural bond of sisters.
But I can tell you that of late this Duke
Hath ta'en displeasure 'gainst his gentle niece,
Grounded upon no other argument
280   But that the people praise her for her virtues,
And pity her for her good father's sake;
And, on my life his malice 'gainst the lady
Will suddenly break forth. Sir, fare you well.
Hereafter, in a better world than this,
285   I shall desire more love and knowledge of you.

Orlando   [*in great frustration*] What emotion has made me so tongue-tied? I can't speak to her, even though she urged me to. Oh, poor Orlando, you are overpowered! Either Charles or someone weaker conquers you. [*By "someone weaker," he refers to* **Rosalind**.]

[**Le Beau** *returns.*]

Le Beau   [*lowering his voice and looking around to make sure no one can overhear*] Good sir, as a friend I advise you to leave this place. Although you deserve great praise, genuine applause, and love, the duke is now in such a state that he misinterprets everything that you have done. The duke is moody. [*He hesitates, not wanting to say too much.*] It's more suitable for you to imagine what he is than for me to tell you.

Orlando   [*shocked but grateful*] Thank you, sir. [*He hesitates but then decides to speak.*] Please tell me this: which of the two ladies that was here at the wrestling was the duke's daughter?

Le Beau   [*dryly*] Judging by manners, neither one is his daughter. But, actually, the shorter one is his daughter; the other is the daughter of the banished duke. She is kept here by her uncle, the usurper, to keep his daughter company. The two ladies' bond of love is stronger than the natural bond between sisters. But I can tell you that lately the duke has begun to be displeased with his gentle niece, based on nothing more than that the people praise her for her good qualities and pity her for the sake of her father. I swear, his hatred for her will soon erupt. [*He looks anxiously over his shoulder once again.*] Sir, farewell. Someday, in a better world than this one, I hope to get to know and love you.

Orlando   I rest much bounden to you; fare you well.

[*Exit* **Le Beau.**]

Thus must I from the smoke into the smother,
From tyrant Duke unto a tyrant brother.
But heavenly Rosalind!

Exit.

Scene 3

Enter **Celia** *and* **Rosalind.**

Celia   Why, cousin, why, Rosalind! Cupid have
mercy, not a word?

Rosalind   Not one to throw at a dog.

Celia   No, thy words are too precious to be cast
away upon curs, throw some of them at me. Come
6   lame me with reasons.

Rosalind   Then there were two cousins laid up, when
the one should be lam'd with reasons, and the other
mad without any.

10 **Celia**   But is all this for your father?

Rosalind   No, some of it is for my child's father. O
how full of briers is this working-day world!

Orlando   I owe you a great deal. Goodbye.

[**Le Beau** *leaves, shaking his head in worry and distress.*]

[*to himself*] So now I must go from a bad situation into a worse one: from a tyrannical duke to a tyrannical brother! But, oh, heavenly Rosalind!

[**Orlando** *leaves.*]

Scene 3

A room in Duke Frederick's palace.

[**Celia** *and* **Rosalind** *enter.*]

Celia   My goodness, Cousin Rosalind! May Cupid have mercy on you! Haven't you a single word to say? [*Cupid was the Roman god of love.*]

Rosalind   [*sighing*] Not even one to throw at a dog. [**Rosalind** *uses a proverbial expression referring to having nothing, not even a scrap of food to throw to a dog.*]

Celia   No, your words are too valuable to be thrown away on dogs. Throw some of them at me. Come on, take your best shot.

Rosalind   Then we would both be sick in bed, one with the blows of reason and the other having lost her ability to reason. [*She refers here to those who would throw rocks at a dog to break its legs.*]

Celia   [*with concern*] But is this all for your father?

Rosalind   No, some of it is for my child's father. [*She is imagining the future when she and* **Orlando** *are married.*] Oh, how full of thorns this everyday world is!

Celia   They are but burs, cousin, thrown upon
thee in holiday foolery; if we walk not in the trod-
15   den paths, our very petticoats will catch them.

Rosalind   I could shake them off my coat; these
burs are in my heart.

Celia   Hem them away.

Rosalind   I would try, if I could cry "hem" and have
20   him.

Celia   Come, come, wrastle with thy affections.

Rosalind   O, they take the part of a better wrastler
than myself!

Celia   O, a good wish upon you! you will try in
25   time, in despite of a fall. But turning these
jests out of service, let us talk in good earnest. Is
it possible, on such a sudden, you should fall into so
strong a liking with old Sir Rowland's youngest son?

Rosalind   The Duke my father lov'd his father
30   dearly.

Celia   Doth it therefore ensue that you should
love his son dearly? By this kind of chase, I should
hate him, for my father hated his father dearly;
yet I hate not Orlando.

35   **Rosalind**   No, faith, hate him not, for my sake.

Celia   Why should I not? Doth he not deserve
well?

Celia   They're only burrs, cousin, thrown at you as a holiday prank. If we stray from well-worn paths, even our petticoats will catch them. [*She means, metaphorically, that behaving unconventionally usually results in having to deal with cultural disapproval, which would be an annoyance similar to having to pull burrs off the hem of one's skirt.*]

Rosalind   I could shake them off if they were on my clothing. These burrs are in my heart.

Celia   Hem them away. [*She puns on "hem," as one hems a garment, as opposed to coughing with an "ahem."*]

Rosalind   I would try it, if I could say "hem" and have him. [*She means that she would cheer up if she could have "him" just by clearing her throat with an "ahem."*]

Celia   Come on, fight your feelings.

Rosalind   Oh, they're on the side of a better wrestler than I!

Celia   [*with twinkling eyes*] Oh, here's a good wish for you: May you wrestle with Orlando even though you'll probably end up on your back. But let's put aside our jokes and have a serious talk. Is it possible that you have fallen in love so suddenly with old Sir Rowland's youngest son, Orlando? [**Celia's** *wish for* **Rosalind** *to wrestle with* **Orlando** *has a double meaning with sexual implications.*]

Rosalind   My father, the duke, loved his father very much.

Celia   [*shaking her head*] Does that necessarily mean that you should love his son very much? By that logic, I should hate him because my father detested his father, yet I don't hate Orlando.

Rosalind   No, really, for my sake don't hate him.

Celia   Why shouldn't I? Doesn't he deserve it?

Enter **Duke [Frederick]** *with* **Lords**.

Rosalind   Let me love him for that, and do you love
him because I do. Look, here comes the Duke.

40 **Celia**   With his eyes full of anger.

Duke Frederick   Mistress, dispatch you with your safest
haste,
And get you from our court.

Rosalind   Me, uncle?

Duke Frederick   You, cousin.
Within these ten days if that thou beest found
So near our public court as twenty miles,
Thou diest for it.

45 **Rosalind**   I do beseech your Grace
Let me the knowledge of my fault bear with me:
If with myself I hold intelligence,
Or have acquaintance with mine own desires;
If that I do not dream or be not frantic
50 (As I do trust I am not), then, dear uncle,
Never so much as in a thought unborn
Did I offend your Highness.

Duke Frederick   Thus do all traitors:
If their purgation did consist in words,
They are as innocent as grace itself.
55 Let it suffice thee that I trust thee not.

Rosalind   Yet your mistrust cannot make me a traitor.
Tell me whereon the [likelihood] depends.

Duke Frederick   Thou art thy father's daughter, there's
enough.

[**Duke Frederick** *and* **Lords** *enter.*]

Rosalind   Let me love him because he deserves it, and you may love him because I do. Look, here comes the duke.

Celia   [*with concern*] He's looking very angry.

Duke Frederick   [*coldly, to* **Rosalind**] Madam, you must leave my palace as quickly as possible.

Rosalind   [*shocked*] Me, Uncle?

Duke Frederick   You, Niece. If, ten days from now, you are seen within twenty miles of this court, you will die.

Rosalind   [*pleadingly*] I beg you, Your Grace, tell me what I have done wrong. If I have any understanding of my thoughts and desires, if I'm not having a bad dream or haven't lost my mind—as I know that I haven't—then, dear uncle, I have never had so much as a passing thought that would have offended you, Your Highness.

Duke Frederick   [*sneeringly*] Exactly what all traitors say. If their innocence depended on what they say, they would all be as innocent as God himself. Let us just say that I don't trust you.

Rosalind   Yet your mistrust alone doesn't make me a traitor. Tell me what reason you have to suspect me.

Duke Frederick   [*snarling*] You are your father's daughter. That's reason enough.

Rosalind   So was I when your Highness took his duke-
     dom,
60   So was I when your Highness banish'd him.
     Treason is not inherited, my lord,
     Or if we did derive it from our friends,
     What's that to me? my father was no traitor.
     Then, good my liege, mistake me not so much
65   To think my poverty is treacherous.

Celia   Dear sovereign, hear me speak.

Duke Frederick   Ay, Celia, we stay'd her for your sake,
     Else had she with her father rang'd along.

Celia   I did not then entreat to have her stay,
70   It was your pleasure and your own remorse.
     I was too young that time to value her,
     But now I know her. If she be a traitor,
     Why so am I. We still have slept together,
     Rose at an instant, learn'd, play'd, eat together,
75   And wheresoe'er we went, like Juno's swans,
     Still we went coupled and inseparable.

Duke Frederick   She is too subtle for thee, and her smooth-
     ness,
     Her very silence, and her patience
     Speak to the people, and they pity her.
80   Thou art a fool; she robs thee of thy name,
     And thou wilt show more bright and seem more vir-
     tuous
     When she is gone. Then open not thy lips:
     Firm and irrevocable is my doom
     Which I have pass'd upon her; she is banish'd.

Celia   Pronounce that sentence then on me, my liege,
86   I cannot live out of her company.

Rosalind   Just as I was when Your Highness took my father's dukedom, as I was when Your Highness banished him. Treason is not inherited, My Lord. Or even if it is inherited from our relatives, what does that have to do with me? My father wasn't a traitor. Then, My Good Ruler, don't be so mistaken as to believe that my poverty has made me disloyal.

Celia   Dear Ruler, please let me speak.

Duke Frederick   Yes, Celia, we allowed her to stay for your sake, or else she would have been sent away with her father.

Celia   I didn't beg then that she be allowed to stay; it was because you wanted her to stay and because you felt guilty. I was too young at that time to fully appreciate her, but now I do know her. If she is a traitor, why, so am I. We have slept together, gotten up at the same time, studied, played, eaten together. And wherever we went, like Juno's swans, we were always together and not to be parted. [*Juno was the Roman goddess of marriage; Shakespeare's image is that of Juno's chariot being drawn by swans.*]

Duke Frederick   She's too devious for you, and her smoothness, even her silence and her patience win the approval of the people, and they feel sorry for her. You're a fool. She steals the good opinion that you should have. Your reputation will be brighter and you will seem more admirable when she is gone. So don't say any more. My judgment on her is firm and will not be changed; she is banished.

Celia   [*weeping*] Then pass that sentence on me, My Ruler. I can't live without her.

Duke Frederick   You are a fool. You, niece, provide your-
  self;
If you outstay the time, upon mine honor,
And in the greatness of my word, you die.

Exit **Duke** [*with* **Lords**].

Celia   O my poor Rosalind, whither wilt thou go?
91   Wilt thou change fathers? I will give thee mine.
I charge thee be not thou more griev'd than I am.

Rosalind   I have more cause.

Celia   Thou hast not, cousin,
Prithee be cheerful. Know'st thou not the Duke
Hath banish'd me, his daughter?

95   **Rosalind**   That he hath not.

Celia   No, hath not? Rosalind lacks then the love
Which teacheth thee that thou and I am one.
Shall we be sund'red? shall we part, sweet girl?
No, let my father seek another heir.
100   Therefore devise with me how we may fly,
Whither to go, and what to bear with us,
And do not seek to take your change upon you,
To bear your griefs yourself, and leave me out;
For by this heaven, now at our sorrows pale,
105   Say what thou canst, I'll go along with thee.

Rosalind   Why, whither shall we go?

Celia   To seek my uncle in the forest of Arden.

Rosalind   Alas, what danger will it be to us,
Maids as we are, to travel forth so far!
110   Beauty provoketh thieves sooner than gold.

Duke Frederick   [*in great disgust*] You're a fool.

[*to* **Rosalind**] You, Niece, make your preparations. If you are still here after the deadline, I swear to you on my honor and on my word as duke, you will die.

[**Duke Frederick** *and* **Lords** *leave.*]

Celia   Oh, my poor Rosalind, where will you go? Will you exchange fathers with me? I'll give you mine. I urge you, don't be more distressed than I am.

Rosalind   I have more reason to be.

Celia   No, you haven't, Cousin. Please cheer up. Don't you see that the duke has banished me, his daughter?

Rosalind   No, he hasn't.

Celia   [*shocked at what she is hearing*] No, he hasn't? Then your love hasn't taught you that you and I are one. Should we be separated? Should we part, sweet girl? No! My father may look for another heir to his kingdom. Therefore, let's plan how we may escape, where we shall go, and what we shall take with us. Don't try to hold up under your bad luck by yourself, bearing your troubles yourself and leaving me out. For, by heaven, which is pale with sorrow at our troubles, say whatever you like, I'll go with you.

Rosalind   Why, where shall we go?

Celia   [*with sudden inspiration*] To look for your father in the Forest of Arden!

Rosalind   But that will be very dangerous for us, young girls that we are, to travel so far! Criminals are even more tempted by beauty than they are by gold.

Celia   I'll put myself in poor and mean attire,
And with a kind of umber smirch my face;
The like do you. So shall we pass along
And never stir assailants.

Rosalind   Were it not better,
115 Because that I am more than common tall,
That I did suit me all points like a man?
A gallant curtle-axe upon my thigh,
A boar-spear in my hand, and—in my heart
Lie there what hidden woman's fear there will—
120 We'll have a swashing and a martial outside,
As many other mannish cowards have
That do outface it with their semblances.

Celia   What shall I call thee when thou art a
man?

Rosalind   I'll have no worse a name than Jove's own
page,
125 And therefore look you call me Ganymed.
But what will you [be] call'd?

Celia   Something that hath a reference to my state:
No longer Celia, but Aliena.

Rosalind   But, cousin, what if we assay'd to steal
130 The clownish fool out of your father's court?
Would he not be a comfort to our travel?

Celia   He'll go along o'er the wide world with me;
Leave me alone to woo him. Let's away,
And get our jewels and our wealth together,
135 Devise the fittest time and safest way
To hide us from pursuit that will be made
After my flight. Now go [we in] content
To liberty, and not to banishment.

Exeunt.

Celia   I'll put on humble and inexpensive clothing and stain my face with brown dye. You do the same. That way we may travel about and not attract any criminals.

Rosalind   [*getting into the spirit of the adventure*] Wouldn't it be better, since I am unusually tall, to dress myself like a man? I could carry an impressive sword at my side, a boar-spear in my hand, and—no matter what feminine fears might hide in my heart—I'll maintain a swaggering and bold appearance, as other cowards do when pretending to have manly courage in order to face down someone.

Celia   What should I call you when you are a man?

Rosalind   I'll have no lesser name than that of Jove's own attendant, so call me Ganymede. But what will you be called? [*In Roman mythology, Jove (also called Jupiter), in the form of an eagle, carried Ganymede, a handsome Trojan prince, to Mount Olympus to be cupbearer to the gods.*]

Celia   [*sighing*] Something that refers to my situation. I'm no longer Celia, but Aliena. [**"Aliena"** *means "estranged one."*]

Rosalind   Cousin, what if we tried to sneak the clownish court jester, Touchstone, out of your father's court? Wouldn't he be a comfort to us as we travel?

Celia   He would go anywhere in the wide world with me. Let me persuade him. Let's go and gather together our jewels and our money, plan the best time and safest way to keep ourselves hidden from the pursuit that will be made after I'm gone. Now we shall happily go to freedom and not to banishment.

[**Rosalind** *and* **Celia** *leave.*]

Act two

Scene 1

Enter **Duke Senior**, **Amiens**, *and two or three* **Lords**, *like foresters.*

Duke Senior   Now, my co-mates and brothers in exile,
Hath not old custom made this life more sweet
Than that of painted pomp? Are not these woods
More free from peril than the envious court?
5   Here feel we not the penalty of Adam,
The seasons' difference, as the icy fang
And churlish chiding of the winter's wind,
Which when it bites and blows upon my body
Even till I shrink with cold, I smile and say,
10   "This is no flattery: these are counsellors
That feelingly persuade me what I am."
Sweet are the uses of adversity,
Which like the toad, ugly and venomous,
Wears yet a precious jewel in his head;
15   And this our life, exempt from public haunt,
Finds tongues in trees, books in the running brooks,
Sermons in stones, and good in every thing.

Amiens   I would not change it. Happy is your Grace,
That can translate the stubbornness of fortune
20   Into so quiet and so sweet a style.

Act two

Scene 1

The Forest of Arden

[**Duke Senior**, **Amiens**, *and two or three* **Lords** *enter, dressed like foresters.*]

Duke Senior [*heartily*] Now, my companions and brothers in exile, since we've grown accustomed to this life, hasn't it become more pleasant than the life of artificial pageantry? Aren't these woods less dangerous than the court is, with all its rivalries? Here we feel only the curse of Adam: the differences in the seasons, such as the icy fangs and bitter harassment of winter's wind. When it bites and blows on my body until I shrink with cold, I smile and say, "This is not flattery; these winds are like advisors that powerfully show me what I really am." Troubles are useful things, like the toad which is ugly and poisonous, yet nevertheless it wears a precious jewel in its forehead. Likewise, in this life, cut off from civilization, the trees speak to us, flowing streams are our books, stones preach sermons to us, and there is good in everything. [*It was commonly believed that the toad had a jewel in its forehead that had the power to heal diseases.*]

Amiens Your Grace is fortunate in being able to transform the uncooperativeness of destiny into such a calm and pleasant state of mind.

Duke Senior   Come, shall we go and kill us venison?
And yet it irks me the poor dappled fools,
Being native burghers of this desert city,
Should in their own confines with forked heads
Have their round haunches gor'd.

First Lord   Indeed, my lord,
26   The melancholy Jaques grieves at that,
And in that kind swears you do more usurp
Than doth your brother that hath banish'd you.
To-day my Lord of Amiens and myself
30   Did steal behind him as he lay along
Under an oak, whose antique root peeps out
Upon the brook that brawls along this wood,
To the which place a poor sequest'red stag,
That from the hunter's aim had ta'en a hurt,
35   Did come to languish; and indeed, my lord,
The wretched animal heav'd forth such groans
That their discharge did stretch his leathern coat
Almost to bursting, and the big round tears
Cours'd one another down his innocent nose
40   In piteous chase; and thus the hairy fool,
Much marked of the melancholy Jaques,
Stood on th' extremest verge of the swift brook,
Augmenting it with tears.

Duke Senior   But what said Jaques?
Did he not moralize this spectacle?

Duke Senior   Come, shall we go and hunt a deer? [*musingly*] And yet it bothers me that the poor, spotted innocents, which are the native citizens of this uninhabited "city," should have their healthy bodies pierced with arrows in their own homes.

First Lord   Actually, My Lord, sorrowful Jaques feels sad about that, and, along the same line of thought, declares that you are a worse usurper than your brother who banished you. Today, Lord Amiens and I crept up behind him as he was lying under an oak, the ancient roots of which push up out of the ground near the noisy brook which flows through this forest. A poor stag, separated from the herd, had been wounded by a hunter and came there to die. In fact, My Lord, the suffering animal sighed out such loud groans that they stretched his hide almost to the point of bursting, and big round tears ran down his innocent nose as if in a race of sorrow, and that was how the innocent beast looked when gloomy Jaques, standing on the very edge of the brook, noticed the deer adding its tears to the stream.

Duke Senior   But what did Jaques say? Didn't he make some moral observation about this sight?

45 **First Lord**   O yes, into a thousand similes.
    First, for his weeping into the needless stream:
    "Poor deer," quoth he, "thou mak'st a testament
    As worldlings do, giving thy sum of more
    To that which had too [much]. Then, being there
      alone,
50   Left and abandoned of his velvet [friends]:
    "'Tis right," quoth he, "thus misery doth part
    The flux of company." Anon a careless herd,
    Full of the pasture, jumps along by him
    And never stays to greet him. "Ay," quoth Jaques,
55   "Sweep on, you fat and greasy citizens,
    'Tis just the fashion. Wherefore do you look
    Upon that poor and broken bankrupt there?"
    Thus most invectively he pierceth through
    The body of [the] country, city, court,
60   Yea, and of this our life, swearing that we
    Are mere usurpers, tyrants, and what's worse,
    To fright the animals and to kill them up
    In their assign'd and native dwelling-place.

    Duke Senior   And did you leave him in this contempla-
      tion?

    Second Lord   We did, my lord, weeping and com-
65   menting
    Upon the sobbing deer.

    Duke Senior   Show me the place.
    I love to cope him in these sullen fits,
    For then he's full of matter.

    First Lord   I'll bring you to him straight.

                                   Exuent.

First Lord   [*chuckling*] Oh, yes, he thought up a thousand comparisons. First, about the deer's weeping into the stream, which didn't need any more water, he said, "Poor deer, you're like the person who writes a will and leaves money to those who have too much already." Then, because it was alone, abandoned by its velvet-coated friends, he said, "That's how it is; poverty separates people from many friends." Just then, a herd, unconcerned about the deer's problems and having just eaten their fill, galloped along past him without even stopping to greet him. "Yes," Jaques said, "Rush past, you fat, greasy citizens. That's exactly what most people do. Why should you look at that poor, broken wretch there?" In that manner he violently cursed, slashing his way through the whole country, the city, the court, yes, and even our life here, declaring that we are nothing but usurpers, tyrants, and even worse things, frightening the animals and killing them in their God-given and natural home.

Duke Senior   And did you leave him in this condition?

Second Lord   [*chuckling*] We did, My Lord. He was still crying and commenting on the sobbing deer.

Duke Senior   [*with dancing eyes*] Show me where he is. I love to debate with him when he is in one of these dismal moods because then he has so much to say.

First Lord   I'll take you to him right away.

[*They all leave.*]

Scene 2

Enter **Duke [Frederick]** *with* **Lords**.

Duke Frederick   Can it be possible that no man saw them?
It cannot be. Some villains of my court
Are of consent and sufferance in this.

First Lord   I cannot hear of any that did see her.
5   The ladies, her attendants of her chamber,
Saw her a-bed, and in the morning early
They found the bed untreasur'd of their mistress.

Second Lord   My lord, the roynish clown, at whom
        so oft
Your Grace was wont to laugh, is also missing.
10   Hisperia, the princess' gentlewoman,
Confesses that she secretly o'erheard
Your daughter and her cousin much commend
The parts and graces of the wrastler
That did but lately foil the sinowy Charles,
15   And she believes, where ever they are gone,
That youth is surely in their company.

Duke Frederick   Send to his brother; fetch that gallant
        hither.
If he be absent, bring his brother to me;
I'll make him find him. Do this suddenly;
20   And let not search and inquisition quail
To bring again these foolish runaways.

                                        Exeunt.

Scene 2

A room in the duke's palace.

[**Duke Frederick** *and two or three* **Lords** *enter.*]

Duke Frederick   [*angry and worried*] Is it possible that no one saw them? It can't be true! Some villains in my court agreed to this and let it happen.

First Lord   I haven't heard that anyone saw her. Her ladies-in-waiting saw her go to bed, and early this morning they found the bed empty.

Second Lord   My lord, that contemptible clown whom you have laughed at so often is also missing. Hisperia, the princess' gentlewoman, has confessed that she secretly overheard your daughter, Celia, and her cousin, Rosalind, enthusiastically praise the talents and accomplishments of the wrestler who just recently defeated the muscular Charles. Hisperia believes that, wherever they have gone, that young man is definitely with them.

Duke Frederick   Send someone to his brother's home. Bring Orlando here. If he isn't there, bring his brother Oliver to me. I'll make him find Orlando. Do this quickly, and don't fail in your searching and inquiries to bring those foolish runaways back.

[**Duke Frederick** *and* **Lords** *leave.*]

Scene 3

Enter **Orlando** *and* **Adam**, [*meeting*].

Orlando   Who's there?

Adam   What, my young master? O my gentle
    master,
    O my sweet master, O you memory
    Of old Sir Rowland! Why, what make you here?
5   Why are you virtuous? Why do people love you?
    And wherefore are you gentle, strong, and valiant?
    Why would you be so fond to overcome
    The bonny priser of the humorous Duke?
    Your praise is come too swiftly home before you.
10   Know you not, master, to [some] kind of men
    Their graces serve them but as enemies?
    No more do yours. Your virtues, gentle master,
    Are sanctified and holy traitors to you.
    O, what a world is this, when what is comely
15   Envenoms him that bears it!

Orlando   Why, what's the matter?

Adam   O unhappy youth,
    Come not within these doors! Within this roof
    The enemy of all your graces lives.
    Your brother—no, no brother, yet the son
20   (Yet not the son, I will not call him son)
    Of him I was about to call his father—
    Hath heard your praises, and this night he means
    To burn the lodging where you use to lie,
    And you within it. If he fail of that,
25   He will have other means to cut you off;
    I overheard him, and his practices.
    This is no place, this house is but a butchery;
    Abhor it, fear it, do not enter it.

Scene 3

In front of Oliver's house.

[**Orlando** *and* **Adam** *enter and meet.*]

Orlando   Who's there?

Adam   [*moaning in agitation and fear*] Is that you, my young
master? Oh, my gentle master! Oh, my sweet master! Oh,
you living memory of old Sir Rowland! What are you doing
here? Why are you so good? Why do people love you? And
why are you noble, strong, and brave? Why were you so
foolish as to defeat the strong champion of the moody
duke? Word of your success has arrived home before you.
Don't you know, master, that some men's virtues only get
them in trouble? That's how yours are: your good qualities,
noble master, have dedicated and devoted themselves to
betraying you. Oh, what a world this is, when that which is
admirable in a person destroys him!

Orlando   [*surprised and alarmed*] Why, what's the matter?

Adam   Oh, you unfortunate young man! Don't come inside
this house. The enemy of all that is good in you lives under
this roof. Your brother Oliver—but no, he's not a true
brother to you, yet he's the son—but not a true son—I won't
call him the son of the man I was about to call his father—
has heard people praising you for winning the wrestling
match, and tonight he intends to burn the house where you
usually sleep, with you in it. If he fails with that, he will find
some other way to kill you. I overheard him and his treacherous plots. This is no place for you; this house is a slaugh-
terhouse. Hate it, fear it, don't come inside it.

Orlando   Why, whither, Adam, wouldst thou have
me go?

Adam   No matter whither, so you come not
30   here.

Orlando   What, wouldst thou have me go and beg my
food?
Or with a base and boist'rous sword enforce
A thievish living on the common road?
This I must do, or know not what to do;
35   Yet this I will not do, do how I can.
I rather will subject me to the malice
Of a diverted blood and bloody brother.

Adam   But do not so. I have five hundred crowns,
The thrifty hire I sav'd under your father,
40   Which I did store to be my foster-nurse,
When service should in my old limbs lie lame,
And unregarded age in corners thrown.
Take that, and He that doth the ravens feed,
Yea, providently caters for the sparrow,
45   Be comfort to my age! Here is the gold,
All this I give you, let me be your servant.
Though I look old, yet I am strong and lusty;
For in my youth I never did apply
Hot and rebellious liquors in my blood,
50   Nor did not with unbashful forehead woo
The means of weakness and debility;
Therefore my age is as a lusty winter,
Frosty, but kindly. Let me go with you,
I'll do the service of a younger man
55   In all your business and necessities.

Orlando   But where should I go then, Adam?

Adam   [*wringing his hands*] It doesn't matter where, as long as you don't come in here.

Orlando   What, do you want me to go and beg for my food? Or use my sword to make my living dishonestly by robbing travelers on the road? That's what I'll have to do, or I don't know what I will do. Yet I won't do that, no matter what happens to me. I would rather stay and put up with the hatred of a bloodthirsty brother who treats me as if we're unrelated.

Adam   Don't do that. I have five hundred crowns that I thriftily saved from my wages your father paid me; I saved it to provide for my care when my old body would be too slow to perform my duties as a servant and would lie forgotten in some corner. Take that money, and may God, who feeds the ravens—yes, and who provides for the sparrow—comfort me in my old age! Here is the gold; I give it all to you. Let me be your servant. Although I look old, I'm still strong and healthy because, when I was young, I never risked my health by drinking heavily, nor did I engage in reckless living. Therefore, my old age is like an invigorating winter, frosty but pleasant. Let me go with you. I'll serve you, just as a younger man would, in any way you need. [**Adam's** *reference to ravens and sparrows refers to Bible passages such as Job 38:41 and Luke 12:6 and 24.*]

Orlando O good old man, how well in thee appears
The constant service of the antique world,
When service sweat for duty, not for meed!
Thou art not for the fashion of these times,
60 Where none will sweat but for promotion,
And having that, do choke their service up
Even with the having. It is not so with thee.
But, poor old man, thou prun'st a rotten tree,
That cannot so much as a blossom yield
65 In lieu of all thy pains and husbandry.
But come thy ways, we'll go along together,
And ere we have thy youthful wages spent,
We'll light upon some settled low content.

Adam Master, go on, and I will follow thee
70 To the last gasp, with truth and loyalty.
From [seventeen] years till now almost fourscore
Here lived I, but now live here no more.
At seventeen years many their fortunes seek,
But at fourscore it is too late a week;
75 Yet fortune cannot recompense me better
Than to die well, and not my master's debtor.

Exeunt.

Orlando   [*deeply touched*] Oh, good old man, you are an example of the faithful service of those in earlier times, when people worked hard out of a sense of duty and not just for their wages! You don't act as others do these days, when no one works hard unless it's to get a promotion, and once they have that, they do the least they can get by with. You're not like that. But, poor old man, you're pruning a rotten tree that can't produce a single blossom in return for all your trouble and care. But, come along. We'll go together, and before we have spent the savings of your youth, we'll figure out how to make a humble living and be content.

Adam   Master, go on, and I'll follow you to my last breath, with truth and loyalty. From the time I was seventeen until now, when I'm almost eighty, I have lived here, but I don't live here any longer. At seventeen, many people go to seek their fortunes, but at eighty it's too late to be doing that. But fortune can't give me a better reward than to die a good death and not owe my master anything.

[**Orlando** *and* **Adam** *leave together.*]

Scene 4

Enter **Rosalind** *for Ganymed,* **Celia** *for Aliena, and*
Clown, alias **Touchstone**.

Rosalind   O Jupiter, how [weary] are my spirits!

Touchstone   I care not for my spirits, if my legs were
not weary.

Rosalind   I could find in my heart to disgrace my
5   man's apparel and to cry like a woman; but I
must comfort the weaker vessel, as doublet and hose
ought to show itself courageous to petticoat; therefore courage, good Aliena.

Celia   I pray you bear with me, I cannot go no
10   further.

Touchstone   For my part, I had rather bear with you
than bear you. Yet I should bear no cross if I did
bear you, for I think you have no money in your
purse.

15 **Rosalind**   Well, this is the forest of Arden.

Touchstone   Ay, now am I in Arden, the more fool I.
When I was at home, I was in a better place, but
travellers must be content.

Scene 4

The Forest of Arden.

[**Rosalind** *dressed as* **Ganymede**, **Celia** *dressed as* **Aliena**, *and* **Touchstone** *enter.*]

Rosalind   [*sighing heavily*] Oh, Jupiter, how weary I am in spirit! [*Jupiter, in Roman mythology, is the chief god.*]

Touchstone   I wouldn't mind about my spirit if my legs weren't so tired.

Rosalind   If it wouldn't bring shame to my man's clothing, I could easily weep like a woman, but I have to comfort the weaker vessel, in the same way that a jacket and hose should demonstrate courage to a skirt. Therefore, have courage, good Aliena! [*"Weaker vessel" means "woman"; see I Peter 3:7. "Hose" refers to the equivalent of men's trousers.*]

Celia   [*sinking to the ground in exhaustion*] Please bear with me. I can't go any farther.

Touchstone   [*punning on "bear" meaning "to carry"*] If it's up to me, I would rather bear with you than carry you. Yet I wouldn't be bearing a cross if I did carry you, for I believe you have no money in your purse. [*Elizabethan pennies had crosses stamped on them.*]

Rosalind   [*looking around*] So this is the Forest of Arden.

Touchstone   Yes, now I'm in Arden, fool that I am. When I was at home, I was in a better place, but travelers must be content with what they get.

Enter **Corin** *and* **Silvius**.

Rosalind   Ay, be so, good Touchstone. Look you,
who comes here, a young man and an old in solemn
21   talk.

Corin   That is the way to make her scorn you still.

Silvius   O Corin, that thou knew'st how I do love her!

Corin   I partly guess; for I have lov'd ere now.

Silvius   No, Corin, being old, thou canst not guess,
26   Though in thy youth thou wast as true a lover
As ever sigh'd upon a midnight pillow.
But if thy love were ever like to mine—
As sure I think did never man love so—
30   How many actions most ridiculous
Hast thou been drawn to by thy fantasy?

Corin   Into a thousand that I have forgotten.

Silvius   O, thou didst then never love so heartily!
If thou rememb'rest not the slightest folly
35   That ever love did make thee run into,
Thou hast not lov'd;
Or if thou hast not sat as I do now,
Wearing thy hearer in thy mistress' praise,
Thou hast not lov'd;
40   Or if thou hast not broke from company
Abruptly, as my passion now makes me,
Thou hast not lov'd.
O Phebe, Phebe, Phebe!

Exit.

Rosalind   Yes, do be content, good Touchstone.

[**Corin** *and* **Silvius** *enter.*]

Look who's coming this way: a young man and an old one in serious conversation.

[**Rosalind**, **Celia**, *and* **Touchstone** *stand off to one side to listen.*]

Corin   [*earnestly*] That's the way to make her keep on despising you.

Silvius   Oh, Corin, if you only knew how much I love her!

Corin   I have a pretty good idea of how you feel. I've been in love before.

Silvius   [*shaking his head*] No, Corin, you're old, so you can't understand, even if, when you were young, you were as devoted a lover as any who ever sighed over his love at midnight in his bed. But if your love ever were like mine— although I'm sure no man has ever loved as I do—How many utterly ridiculous things have you found yourself doing because of your love?

Corin   [*dryly*] I've done at least a thousand that I've forgotten.

Silvius   Then you can never have loved so deeply as I do! If you don't remember the least little foolish thing that love ever made you do, you haven't been in love. Or if you haven't sat, as I'm doing now, wearing out the person listening to you with praising your beloved, then you haven't loved. Or if you haven't suddenly broken away from those you were with, as my feelings now make me do, you haven't loved. Oh, Phebe, Phebe, Phebe!

[**Silvius** *runs off, moaning his beloved's name.*]

Rosalind   Alas, poor shepherd, searching of [thy
    wound],
45 I have by hard adventure found mine own.

Touchstone   And I mine. I remember, when I was
    in love, I broke my sword upon a stone and bid him
    take that for coming a-night to Jane Smile; and I
    remember the kissing of her batler and the cow's
50 dugs that her pretty chopp'd hands had milk'd;
    and I remember the wooing of a peascod instead of
    her, from whom I took two cods, and giving her
    them again, said with weeping tears, "Wear these
    for my sake." We that are true lovers run into
55 strange capers; but as all is mortal in nature,
    so is all nature in love mortal in folly.

Rosalind   Thou speak'st wiser than thou art ware of.

Touchstone   Nay, I shall ne'er be ware of mine own
    wit till I break my shins against it.

60 **Rosalind**   Jove, Jove! this shepherd's passion
    Is much upon my fashion.

Touchstone   And mine, but it grows something stale
    with me.

Celia   I pray you, one of you question yond man,
65 If he for gold will give us any food;
    I faint almost to death.

Touchstone   Holla! you clown!

Rosalind   Peace, fool, he's not thy kinsman.

Corin   Who calls?

Touchstone   Your betters, sir.

Rosalind   Ah, poor shepherd, in looking at your heartache I have, unfortunately, recalled my own.

Touchstone   So have I. I remember when I was in love I broke my sword on a stone and told it to take that for coming at night to see Jane Smile. And I remember kissing the paddle she used for beating clothes while she washed them and the cow's udders that she had milked with her pretty, chapped hands. And I remember wooing, instead of her, a pea plant from which I took two pods and then gave them back to the plant, weeping as I said, "Wear them for my sake." We true lovers do strange things, but just as all things that live must die, the foolishness of love must die also.

Rosalind   What you say is wiser than you are aware.

Touchstone   No, I shall never be wary of my own wit until I hurt my shins running into it. [**Touchstone** *quibbles on the word "ware," which* **Rosalind** *used in the sense of being aware of something, but he refers to being wary or cautious.*]

Rosalind   [*to herself, referring to* **Silvius**] Oh, God! This shepherd's emotional state is almost the same as mine.

Touchstone   And mine, but I'm starting to get tired of it.

Celia   [*faintly*] Would one of you please ask that man over there if we can buy some food from him? I'm so weak I feel like I'm about to die.

Touchstone   [*calling out to* **Corin**, *using a word that was an insulting term for a social inferior*] Hey there, clown!

Rosalind   [*punning on the word "clown"*] Quiet, fool. He's not a jester like you.

Corin   Who is calling?

Touchstone   Your betters, sir.

Corin   Else are they very wretched.

Rosalind   Peace, I say. Good even to [you], friend.

70 **Corin**   And to you, gentle sir, and to you all.

Rosalind   I prithee, shepherd, if that love or gold
Can in this desert place buy entertainment,
Bring us where we may rest ourselves and feed.
Here's a young maid with travel much oppressed,
And faints for succor.

75 **Corin**   Fair sir, I pity her,
And wish, for her sake more than for mine own,
My fortunes were more able to relieve her;
But I am shepherd to another man,
And do not shear the fleeces that I graze.
80 My master is of churlish disposition,
And little reaks to find the way to heaven
By doing deeds of hospitality.
Besides, his cote, his flocks, and bounds of feed
Are now on sale, and at our sheep-cote now
85 By reason of his absence there is nothing
That you will feed on; but what is, come see,
And in my voice most welcome shall you be.

Rosalind   What is he that shall buy his flock and pasture?

Corin   That young swain that you saw here but
erewhile,
90 That little cares for buying any thing.

Rosalind   I pray thee, if it stand with honesty,
Buy thou the cottage, pasture, and the flock,
And thou shalt have to pay for it of us.

Corin   You couldn't be much lower.

Rosalind   [*to* **Touchstone**] I said be quiet.

[*speaking as* **Ganymede** *to* **Corin**] Good evening to you, friend.

Corin   [*tugging the front lock of his hair as was customary when greeting a social superior*] And the same to you, noble sir, and to all of you.

Rosalind   Please tell me, shepherd, if either kindness or gold can get us food and a place to stay out here in this uninhabited place. Bring us to where we may rest ourselves and eat something. [*gesturing toward* **Celia**] This young maiden here is worn out from traveling and faint from hunger.

Corin   Dear sir, I feel sorry for her and wish, for her sake more than for my own, that my fortunes would make it more possible for me to help her. But I work for another man as his shepherd and don't profit from the fleeces of the sheep I tend. My master is stingy and doesn't care about getting into heaven by offering hospitality to others. Besides, his cottage, his flocks, and the pastures for feeding his sheep are now for sale, and because of his absence from the place, there is nothing you would want to eat at his cottage. But come and see what's there, and I will welcome you warmly.

Rosalind   Who is thinking of buying his flock and pasture?

Corin: That young fellow you saw here just now, but he doesn't really care about buying anything.

Rosalind   Please, if you can do so in honesty, buy the cottage, pasture, and the flock, and we will give you the money you need to pay for it.

Celia   And we will mend thy wages. I like this
　　place,
95   And willingly could waste my time in it.

Corin   Assuredly the thing is to be sold.
　　Go with me; if you like upon report
　　The soil, the profit, and this kind of life,
99   I will your very faithful feeder be,
　　And buy it with your gold right suddenly.

Exeunt.

Scene 5

Enter **Amiens**, **Jaques**, *and others.*

SONG

[**Amiens**]　　Under the greenwood tree
　　　　Who loves to lie with me,
　　　　And turn his merry note
　　　　Unto the sweet bird's throat,
5　　　　Come hither, come hither, come hither!
　　　　Here shall he see
　　　　No enemy
　　　　But winter and rough weather.

Jaques   More, more, I prithee more.

Amiens   It will make you melancholy, Monsieur
11   Jaques.

Jaques   I thank it. More, I prithee more. I can
　　suck melancholy out of a song, as a weasel sucks eggs.
　　More, I prithee more.

15 **Amiens**   My voice is ragged, I know I cannot
　　please you.

Celia   And we will increase your wages. I like this place, and I'm willing to spend some time here.

Corin   Oh, it's definitely going to be sold. Go with me, and if, when you've looked things over, you like the land, the profits, and this kind of life, I will be your very faithful servant and buy it with your gold right away.

[**Rosalind**, **Celia**, **Touchstone**, *and* **Corin** *leave together.*]

Scene 5

The Forest of Arden.

[**Amiens**, **Jaques**, *and others enter.*]

Amiens   [*singing*] *Under the greenwood tree*
Whoever loves to lie with me
And tune his happy song
To match the sweet bird's singing,
Come here, come here, come here.
Here he shall find no enemy
But winter and harsh weather.

Jaques   [*clapping enthusiastically*] Sing more! More, please, more!

Amiens   [*shaking his head*] It will make you sad, Monsieur Jaques.

Jaques   I like it. More, please, more. I can suck sadness out of a song like a weasel sucks eggs. More, please, more.

Amiens   My voice is raspy. I know I can't please you with it.

Jaques I do not desire you to please me, I do desire
you to sing. Come, more, another stanzo. Call you
'em stanzos?

20 **Amiens** What you will, Monsieur Jaques.

Jaques Nay, I care not for their names, they owe
me nothing. Will you sing?

Amiens More at your request than to please my-
24 self.

Jaques Well then, if ever I thank any man, I'll
thank you; but that they call compliment is like th'
encounter of two dog-apes; and when a man thanks
me heartily, methinks I have given him a penny, and
he renders me the beggarly thanks. Come, sing;
30 and you that will not, hold your tongues.

Amiens Well, I'll end the song. Sirs, cover the
while; the Duke will drink under this tree. He hath
been all this day to look you.

Jaques And I have been all this day to avoid him.
35 He is too disputable for my company. I think
of as many matters as he, but I give heaven thanks,
and make no boast of them. Come, warble, come.

SONG   *All together here.*

Who doth ambition shun,
   And loves to live i' th' sun,
40   Seeking the food he eats,
    And pleas'd with what he gets,
Come hither, come hither, come hither!
    Here shall he see
    [No enemy
45 But winter and rough weather].

Jaques   I don't want you to please me; I want you to sing.
Come, more. Sing another stanza. Do you call them "stanzas"?

Amiens   Call them whatever you like, Monsieur Jaques.

Jaques   No, I don't care what their names are; they don't
owe me anything. Will you sing? [**Jaques** *quibbles on*
"nomen," the Latin word for "name," which could be used
to mean "debtor."]

Amiens   I'll do it because you asked, not to please myself.

Jaques   Well, then, if I ever thank anyone, I'll thank you. But
what people call formal courtesy is no better than two
baboons greeting one another. Whenever a man thanks me
heartily, it reminds me of when I've given a beggar a penny
and he thanks me excessively. Come, sing.

[*calling to the others present*] And those of you who won't
sing, be quiet.

Amiens   Well, I'll finish the song.

[*to the others present*] Sirs, while I sing, set the table. The
duke will dine under this tree.

[*to* **Jaques**] He has been looking for you all day.

Jaques   And I've been avoiding him all day. He is too fond
of debating for my taste. I think of just as many issues as he
does, but I just thank heaven that I do, and don't brag about
them. Come, warble, come.

Amiens *and* **Others**   [*singing*] *Whoever rejects ambition*
    And loves to live in the sun
    Hunting the food he eats
    And contented with what he gets,
    Come here, come here, come here.
    Here he shall find no enemy
    But winter and harsh weather.

Jaques   I'll give you a verse to this note, that I made
yesterday in despite of my invention.

Amiens   And I'll sing it.

[Jaques]   Thus it goes:

50   If it do come to pass
                     That any man turn ass,
                     Leaving his wealth and ease
                     A stubborn will to please,
              Ducdame, ducdame, ducdame!
55   Here shall he see
                     Gross fools as he,
                 And if he will come to me.

Amiens   What's that "ducdame"?

Jaques   'Tis a Greek invocation, to call fools into a
circle. I'll go sleep, if I can; if I cannot, I'll rail
61   against all the first-born of Egypt.

Amiens   And I'll go seek the Duke, his banket is pre-
par'd.

Exeunt.

Jaques   I'll give you a verse to this tune that I wrote yesterday, in spite of my lack of creativity.

Amiens   And I'll sing it.

Jaques   Here's how it goes:

[*singing*] *If it should come to pass*
             That a man acts like an ass
             And leaves his wealth and comfort
             Because he is so stubborn,
             Ducdame, ducdame, ducdame.
             Here he will see
             Fools as stupid as he,
             If only he will come to me.

Amiens   What's that word "ducdame"? [*Experts do not
agree about the meaning or derivation of the word (which
is pronounced with three syllables). Shakespeare may have
invented it.*]

Jaques   [*Many productions have the others present gather
in a circle around* **Jaques** *as he sings.*] It's a magical word
used to call fools together into a circle. I'm going to take a
nap, if I can. If I can't, I'll curse all the first-born of Egypt.
[*"The first-born of Egypt" refers to the killing of the first-
born of Egypt by the Angel of Death, as recorded in Exodus
12:29-30. The word "gypsy" derives from the word "Egypt-
ian," so* **Jaques** *may be saying he'll curse his fellow exiles
who, like gypsies, are vagabonds.*]

Amiens   And I'll go look for the duke. His meal is ready.

[**Jaques** *and* **Amiens** *leave separately.*]

Scene 6

Enter **Orlando** *and* **Adam**.

Adam   Dear master, I can go no further. O, I die
for food! Here lie I down, and measure out my grave.
Farewell, kind master.

Orlando   Why, how now, Adam? no greater heart in
5   thee? Live a little, comfort a little, cheer thyself a little. If this uncouth forest yield any thing
savage, I will either be food for it, or bring it for
food to thee. Thy conceit is nearer death than
thy powers. For my sake be comfortable, hold
10   death a while at the arm's end. I will here be with
thee presently, and if I bring thee not something to
eat, I will give thee leave to die; but if thou diest
before I come, thou art a mocker of my labor. Well
said, thou look'st cheerly, and I'll be with thee
15   quickly. Yet thou liest in the bleak air. Come,
I will bear thee to some shelter, and thou shalt not
die for lack of a dinner if there live any thing in this
desert. Cheerly, good Adam!

Exeunt.

Scene 6

The Forest of Arden.

[**Orlando** *and* **Adam** *enter.*]

Adam   [*sinking to the ground in exhaustion*] Dear master, I can go no farther. Oh, I'm dying from hunger! I'll lie down here and measure out my grave. Goodbye, kind master.

Orlando   Why, what do you mean, Adam? Have you no courage left? Live a little, comfort yourself a little, encourage yourself a little. If I can find any savage beast in this wild forest, I will either be food for it or bring it back as food for you. You think you're nearer death than you really are. For my sake, cheer up. Hold death at arm's length for a while. I'll come back soon, and if I don't bring you something to eat, I'll give you permission to die. But if you die before I return, you'll have wasted my efforts. [**Adam** *chuckles weakly.*] There you go! You're looking more cheerful, and I'll be back soon. [**Orlando** *suddenly notices how cold it is.*] But you're lying in the cold air. Come, I'll carry you to some shelter. And you won't die for lack of dinner if there is any living thing in this deserted place. Cheer up, good Adam!

[**Orlando** *carries* **Adam** *out.*]

Scene 7

[A table set out.] Enter **Duke Senior**, [**Amiens**], *and*
Lord[s], *like outlaws.*

Duke Senior   I think he be transform'd into a beast,
For I can no where find him like a man.

First Lord   My lord, he is but even now gone hence;
Here was he merry, hearing of a song.

5 **Duke Senior**   If he, compact of jars, grow musical,
We shall have shortly discord in the spheres.
Go seek him, tell him I would speak with him.

Enter **Jaques**.

First Lord   He saves my labor by his own approach.

Duke Senior   Why, how now, monsieur, what a life is
this,
10 That your poor friends must woo your company?
What, you look merrily!

Scene 7

The Forest of Arden.

[**Duke Senior, Amiens,** *and* **Lords,** *all dressed as outlaws, enter. A table is set for a meal.*]

Duke Senior   I think Jaques must have been turned into an animal, for I can't find him anywhere in the form of a man.

First Lord   My Lord, he just left here. He was in a good mood here, listening to a song.

Duke Senior   If he, composed of nothing but sour notes, becomes musical, we shall soon have the whole universe out of harmony. Go, look for him. Tell him I want to talk to him. [*At one time, people thought that the planets and stars revolve around the earth within transparent spheres which make a beautiful harmony that cannot be heard by humans.*]

[**Jaques** *enters.*]

First Lord   He has saved me the trouble. Here he is.

Duke Senior   Why, there you are, Monsieur. What kind of life is this, that your poor friends must plead for your company? [*Noticing* **Jaques'** *expression,* **Duke Senior** *exclaims in surprise.*] Why, you look cheerful!

Jaques   A fool, a fool! I met a fool i' th' forest,
A motley fool. A miserable world!
As I do live by food, I met a fool,
15   Who laid him down, and bask'd him in the sun,
And rail'd on Lady Fortune in good terms,
In good set terms, and yet a motley fool.
"Good morrow, fool," quoth I. "No, sir," quoth he,
"Call me not fool till heaven hath sent me fortune."
20   And then he drew a dial from his poke,
And looking on it, with lack-lustre eye,
Says very wisely, "It is ten a' clock.
Thus we may see," quoth he, "how the world wags.
'Tis but an hour ago since it was nine,
25   And after one hour more 'twill be eleven,
And so, from hour to hour, we ripe and ripe,
And then, from hour to hour, we rot and rot;
And thereby hangs a tale." When I did hear
The motley fool thus moral on the time,
30   My lungs began to crow like chanticleer,
That fools should be so deep contemplative;
And I did laugh sans intermission
An hour by his dial. O noble fool!
A worthy fool! Motley's the only wear.

35 **Duke Senior**   What fool is this?

Jaques   O worthy fool! One that hath been a courtier,
And says, if ladies be but young and fair,
They have the gift to know it; and in his brain,
Which is as dry as the remainder biscuit
40   After a voyage, he hath strange places cramm'd
With observation, the which he vents
In mangled forms. O that I were a fool!
I am ambitious for a motley coat.

Duke Senior   Thou shalt have one.

Jaques [*laughing in delight*] A fool, a fool! I met a fool in
the forest. He was wearing a jester's outfit. What a miserable world! As surely as I eat food to stay alive, I met a fool
who was lying down, relaxing in the sun. He was complain-
ing about his fortune—in formally composed lines, in fact—
yet he was still a fool. "Good day, fool," I said. "No, sir," he
said, "don't call me a fool until heaven has sent me good
fortune." [*He refers to the old saying, "Fortune favors
fools," meaning that fools have the best luck.*] And then he
pulled a watch out of his pouch, and, looking at it with a
dreary eye, he said very wisely, "It's ten o'clock. And that
shows us," he said, "how the world staggers along. Just an
hour ago, it was nine, and in another hour it will be eleven.
And so, from one hour to the next, we get riper and riper,
and then from one hour to the next, we rot away. And that's
the story." When I heard the motley fool moralizing on the
meaning of time, I laughed as loudly as a rooster crowing
to think that fools should meditate so deeply. And I've been
laughing nonstop for an hour, according to his clock. Oh,
what a noble fool! What a praiseworthy fool! Motley is the
only thing to wear. [*Jesters traditionally wore a multicol-
ored garment called "motley."*]

Duke Senior Who is this fool?

Jaques Oh, what a praiseworthy fool! He has been a
courtier, and he says, "If ladies are young and beautiful,
they are well aware of it." And his brain, which is as dry as
the leftover bread from a long sea voyage, has strange
crannies crammed with thoughts which he spouts, all
mangled up. Oh, I wish I were a fool! I wish I had the
jester's motley. [*A "dry" brain was associated with good
memory.*]

Duke Senior You shall have it.

Jaques   It is my only suit—
45   Provided that you weed your better judgments
        Of all opinion that grows rank in them
        That I am wise. I must have liberty
        Withal, as large a charter as the wind,
        To blow on whom I please, for so fools have;
50   And they that are most galled with my folly,
        They most must laugh. And why, sir, must they so?
        The why is plain as way to parish church:
        He that a fool doth very wisely hit
        Doth very foolishly, although he smart,
55   [Not to] seem senseless of the bob; if not,
        The wise man's folly is anatomiz'd
        Even by the squand'ring glances of the fool.
        Invest me in my motley; give me leave
        To speak my mind, and I will through and through
60   Cleanse the foul body of th' infected world,
        If they will patiently receive my medicine.

        Duke Senior   Fie on thee! I can tell what thou wouldst
            do.

        Jaques   What, for a counter, would I do but good?

        Duke Senior   Most mischievous foul sin, in chiding sin:
65   For thou thyself hast been a libertine,
        As sensual as the brutish sting itself,
        And all th' embossed sores, and headed evils,
        That thou with license of free foot hast caught,
        Wouldst thou disgorge into the general world.

Jaques   It's the suit that suits me, so long as you weed out
from among your valid opinions any wild idea that I am
wise. I must also be as free as the wind that blows to sati-
rize anyone I want to, for that's what fools do. And those
who are most annoyed by my foolishness will laugh the
hardest. And why, sir, will they laugh? The reason is as
obvious as the well-worn path to the parish church: He who
is wittily mocked by a fool behaves very foolishly if he
doesn't pretend that what the fool says doesn't upset him. If
he doesn't do so, the random jokes of the fool will appear
to specifically reveal the foolish things the wise man has
done. Let me wear the clothing of the fool, and allow me to
say what's on my mind. I will clean out the infections of this
sick world if people will just take my medicine.

Duke Senior   [*sternly*] Shame on you! I know what you
would do.

Jaques   I'll give you a counter if you can tell me what,
besides good, I would do. [*A counter is a worthless coin.*
Jaques *is saying that the duke's opinion is worthless, like
the counter.*]

Duke Senior   [*in disgust*] Who are you, vile sinner, to scold
sinners? You yourself have been an immoral person, as
lustful as the sexual appetite itself. You would just spew out
on everyone else all the bulging sores and swollen boils of
sin that you have been infected with because of your own
rampant immoral living.

70 **Jaques**   Why, who cries out on pride
       That can therein tax any private party?
       Doth it not flow as hugely as the sea,
       Till that the weary very means do ebb?
       What woman in the city do I name,
75   When that I say the city-woman bears
       The cost of princes on unworthy shoulders?
       Who can come in and say that I mean her,
       When such a one as she, such is her neighbor?
       Or what is he of basest function,
80   That says his bravery is not of my cost,
       Thinking that I mean him, but therein suits
       His folly to the mettle of my speech?
       There then! how then? what then? Let me see
         wherein
       My tongue hath wrong'd him; if it do him right,
85   Then he hath wrong'd himself. If he be free,
       Why then my taxing like a wild goose flies,
       Unclaim'd of any man. But who [comes] here?

Enter **Orlando** [*with his sword drawn*].

Orlando   Forbear, and eat no more.

Jaques   Why, I have eat none yet.

Orlando   Nor shalt not, till necessity be serv'd.

90 **Jaques**   Of what kind should this cock come of?

Duke Senior   Art thou thus bolden'd, man, by thy dis-
      tress?
      Or else a rude despiser of good manners,
      That in civility thou seem'st so empty?

Jaques [*Ignoring what the duke has said,* **Jaques** *continues his justification of satire.*] Why, how can he who speaks
in general against those who flaunt their expensive possessions be said to attack any particular person? Won't it continue to be a problem as enormous as the ocean, until the
wealth that causes the problem is exhausted by uncon-
trolled spending and ebbs away like the tide? What particular woman in the city do I specify when I say that the
citizen's wife wears the fancy clothing of nobility on her
unworthy back? Who can complain that I mean her when
she is just as bad as her neighbor? Or what person of the
lowest occupation, in assuming that I'm talking about him,
can ask what right I have to object to his expensive clothes
since they don't cost me anything without admitting that
his foolishness is what I'm talking about? So there then,
how about that? Show me how I have injured him by what
I've said. If he has it coming, then he has harmed himself. If
he doesn't deserve what I've said, then my satire is like a
wild goose in flight that belongs to no one, in that it doesn't
apply to him.

[**Orlando** *enters with his sword drawn.*]

But who is this?

Orlando [*threateningly*] Stop, and don't eat anything more!

Jaques Why, I haven't eaten anything yet.

Orlando Nor shall you, until my needs are met.

Jaques [*in amusement*] What kind of fighting rooster is
this?

Duke Senior [*courteously but sternly*] Is it your hardship,
man, that is causing you to act so boldly, or do you act so
rudely because you despise good manners?

Orlando   You touch'd my vein at first. The thorny point
95   Of bare distress hath ta'en from me the show
Of smooth civility; yet am I inland bred,
And know some nurture. But forbear, I say,
He dies that touches any of this fruit
Till I and my affairs are answered.

Jaques   And you will not be answer'd with reason,
101   I must die.

Duke Senior   What would you have? Your gentleness shall force,
More than your force move us to gentleness.

Orlando   I almost die for food, and let me have it.

Duke Senior   Sit down and feed, and welcome to our
105   table.

Orlando   Speak you so gently? Pardon me, I pray you.
I thought that all things had been savage here,
And therefore put I on the countenance
Of stern command'ment. But what e'er you are
110   That in this desert inaccessible,
Under the shade of melancholy boughs,
Lose and neglect the creeping hours of time;
If ever you have look'd on better days,
If ever been where bells have knoll'd to church,
115   If ever sate at any good man's feast,
If ever from your eyelids wip'd a tear,
And know what 'tis to pity, and be pitied,
Let gentleness my strong enforcement be,
In the which hope I blush, and hide my sword.

Orlando   Your first guess about my condition was correct; the sharp sting of trouble has stripped me of the appearance of mild courtesy, yet I was reared in civilized society and have had some education. [*He resumes his threatening tone and brandishes his sword.*] But stop, I say! Whoever eats any of this fruit, until I and my business are taken care of, dies.

Jaques   If you won't be satisfied with reason, I'll have to die. [**Jaques**, *popping a grape into his mouth, puns on "reason" and "raisin," which were closer in pronunciation then than now.*]

Duke Senior   [*gesturing invitingly toward the food*] What would you like? Your courtesy will be more forceful than using force to cause us to be compassionate.

Orlando   I'm nearly dead from hunger. Let me have it.

Duke Senior   Sit down and eat. You are welcome at our table.

Orlando   You're speaking to me so politely? Forgive me, please. I thought that everything here would be uncivilized; that's why I pretended to be so grimly commanding. But whoever you are, who lose track of time's slowly passing hours under the shade of the dismal tree branches in this forbidding wilderness, if you have ever seen better times or been where the tolling bells called people to church, if you've ever sat at any good man's table to feast or ever wiped away a tear from your eyes and known what it is to have pity or to be pitied by someone, let my courteous manners strongly compel you. Hoping that will be the case, I blush at the way I've acted and put away my sword. [*He slowly sheaths his sword.*]

Duke Senior   True is it that we have seen better days,
121   And have with holy bell been knoll'd to church,
And sat at good men's feasts, and wip'd our eyes
Of drops that sacred pity hath engend'red;
And therefore sit you down in gentleness,
125   And take upon command what help we have
That to your wanting may be minist'red.

Orlando   Then but forbear your food a little while,
Whiles, like a doe, I go to find my fawn,
And give it food. There is an old poor man,
130   Who after me hath many a weary step
Limp'd in pure love; till he be first suffic'd,
Oppress'd with two weak evils, age and hunger,
I will not touch a bit.

Duke Senior   Go find him out,
And we will nothing waste till you return.

Orlando   I thank ye, and be blest for your good com-
135   fort!

[*Exit.*]

Duke Senior   Thou seest we are not all alone unhappy:
This wide and universal theatre
Presents more woeful pageants than the scene
Wherein we play in.

Duke Senior   It's true that we have seen better days, and have been called to church by holy bell, and sat at the feasts of good men, and wiped away the tears from our eyes that sacred pity has caused. Therefore, sit down in courtesy, and you may command our help to provide for your needs.

Orlando   Please, then, put off your eating for a little while, while I like a mother deer go to find my fawn and give it food. There is an old, poor man who has wearily limped a long distance after me out of pure love. He is afflicted with two terrible weaknesses, age and hunger, and until he is provided for, I will not eat a bite.

Duke Senior   Go find him. We will not eat anything until you return.

Orlando   Thank you, and may you be blessed for your kindness!

[**Orlando** *leaves.*]

Duke Senior   You see that we are not the only ones to be unfortunate. This wide, universal theater puts on more tragic plays than just the scene in which we act.

Jaques   All the world's a stage,
140   And all the men and women merely players;
       They have their exits and their entrances,
       And one man in his time plays many parts,
       His acts being seven ages. At first the infant,
       Mewling and puking in the nurse's arms.
145   Then the whining schoolboy, with his satchel
       And shining morning face, creeping like snail
       Unwillingly to school. And then the lover,
       Sighing like furnace, with a woeful ballad
       Made to his mistress' eyebrow. Then a soldier,
150   Full of strange oaths, and bearded like the pard,
       Jealous in honor, sudden, and quick in quarrel,
       Seeking the bubble reputation
       Even in the cannon's mouth. And then the justice,
       In fair round belly with good capon lin'd,
155   With eyes severe and beard of formal cut,
       Full of wise saws and modern instances;
       And so he plays his part. The sixt age shifts
       Into the lean and slipper'd pantaloon,
       With spectacles on nose, and pouch on side,
160   His youthful hose, well sav'd, a world too wide
       For his shrunk shank, and his big manly voice,
       Turning again toward childish treble, pipes
       And whistles in his sound. Last scene of all,
       That ends this strange eventful history,
165   Is second childishness and mere oblivion,
       Sans teeth, sans eyes, sans taste, sans every thing.

Enter **Orlando** *with* **Adam**.

Duke Senior   Welcome. Set down your venerable bur-
       then,
And let him feed.

Orlando   I thank you most for him.

Jaques   The entire world is a stage, and all the men and women are merely actors. They make their exits and their entrances, and each man during his lifetime plays many parts, with his life divided into in seven acts. At first, he's an infant, whimpering and puking in the wet nurse's arms. Then, he's a whining schoolboy, with his book bag and freshly washed face, creeping reluctantly to school like a snail. Then he's the lover, sighing as gustily as a furnace belching out smoke, writing a mournful poem on the subject of his girlfriend's eyebrows. Then he's a soldier, cursing in foreign languages and with a long mustache like the whiskers of a leopard, fiercely protective of his honor and overly quick to fight, risking cannon fire in order to gain fame, which is no more lasting than a bubble. And then he's the judge, with a nice round belly stuffed with roasted chicken—from all the bribes he's taken. He has stern eyes and a neatly trimmed beard, and he's always quoting wise sayings and using clichéd illustrations; that's how he performs his part. For his sixth role, he becomes the stock character, the foolish old man, skinny and wearing slippers, eyeglasses on his nose and his moneybag hanging from his belt. He still wears the trousers he wore as a young man because he has carefully preserved them, but now they are miles too wide for his skinny legs, and his big, booming voice, becoming as high-pitched as that of a child, squeaks and whistles as he talks. The last scene of all, the one that ends this odd, eventful play, is a second childhood and utter loss of memory: without teeth, without eyesight, without taste, without everything.

[**Orlando** *returns carrying* **Adam**.]

Duke Senior   [*graciously*] Welcome. Set down your honorable burden and let him eat.

Orlando   I thank you very much on his behalf.

Adam   So had you need,
170 I scarce can speak to thank you for myself.

Duke Senior Welcome, fall to. I will not trouble you
As yet to question you about your fortunes.
Give us some music, and, good cousin, sing.

SONG

[Amiens]   Blow, blow, thou winter wind,
175   Thou art not so unkind
                              As man's ingratitude;
                         Thy tooth is not so keen,
                         Because thou art not seen,
                              Although thy breath be rude.
180   Heigh-ho, sing, heigh-ho! unto the green holly,
          Most friendship is feigning, most loving mere folly.
                         [Then] heigh-ho, the holly!
                            This life is most jolly.
                         Freeze, freeze, thou bitter sky,

185   That dost not bite so nigh
                              As benefits forgot;
                         Though thou the waters warp,
                         Thy sting is not so sharp
                              As friend rememb'red not.
190   Heigh-ho, sing, etc.

Adam   [*weakly but sincerely*] You need to do so; I can barely speak to thank you myself.

Duke Senior   [*to* **Adam**] Welcome. Start eating. I won't bother you just now to ask you about what has happened to you.

[*to others*] Play some music.

[*to* **Amiens**] And, good friend, sing for us.

Amiens   [*singing*] *Blow, blow, winter wind,*
        You are not as unkind
        As the ingratitude of humanity.
        Your teeth are not as sharp
        Because you can't be seen,
        Although you blow so fiercely.
        Heigh-ho! Sing, heigh-ho to the green holly.
        Most friendship is false, most love is just foolish.
        Then, heigh-ho, the holly!
        This life is very jolly.

        Freeze, freeze, frigid sky.
        Your bite is not as painful
        As the hurt of kindnesses forgotten.
        Although you can freeze water,
        You do not sting like the pain
        Of a friend who has forgotten one.
        Heigh-ho! Sing, heigh-ho to the green holly.
        Most friendship is false, most love is just foolish.
        Then, heigh-ho, the holly!
        This life is very jolly.

Duke Senior   If that you were the good Sir Rowland's
    son,
    As you have whisper'd faithfully you were,
    And as mine eye doth his effigies witness
    Most truly limn'd and living in your face,
195   Be truly welcome hither. I am the Duke
    That lov'd your father. The residue of your fortune,
    Go to my cave and tell me. Good old man,
    Thou art right welcome as thy [master] is.
    Support him by the arm. Give me your hand,
200   And let me all your fortunes understand.

Exeunt.

Duke Senior   If you really are good Sir Rowland's son, as
you have whispered to me, assuring me that you are and as
I can see by the strong resemblance, drawn like a living
witness in your face, you are truly welcome here. I am the
duke who loved your father. Come into my cave and tell me
the rest of what has happened to you.

[*to* **Adam**] Good old man, you are as welcome as your
master is.

[*to* **Orlando**] Give him your arm.

[*to* **Adam**] Give me your hand and tell me everything that has
happened to you.

[*Everyone on stage leaves.*]

Act three

Scene 1

Enter **Duke [Frederick]**, **Lords**, *and* **Oliver**.

Duke Frederick   Not see him since? Sir, sir, that cannot
    be.
But were I not the better part made mercy,
I should not seek an absent argument
Of my revenge, thou present. But look to it:
5 Find out thy brother, wheresoe'er he is;
Seek him with candle; bring him dead or living
Within this twelvemonth, or turn thou no more
To seek a living in our territory.
Thy lands and all things that thou dost call thine
10 Worth seizure do we seize into our hands,
Till thou canst quit thee by thy brother's mouth
Of what we think against thee.

    Oliver   O that your Highness knew my heart in this!
I never lov'd my brother in my life.

Duke Frederick   More villain thou. Well, push him out
15 of doors,
And let my officers of such a nature
Make an extent upon his house and lands.
Do this expediently, and turn him going.

Exeunt.

Act three

Scene 1

A room in the duke's palace

[**Duke Frederick**, **Oliver**, *and two or three* **Lords** *enter.*]

Duke Frederick   [*with strong skepticism and impatience*]
You haven't seen him since then? Sir, sir, that can't be true!
If I weren't such a merciful man, I wouldn't bother to look
for your missing brother Orlando as a target for my
revenge; I would punish you instead since you are here. But
this is what you must do: Find your brother, wherever he is.
Hunt for him as diligently as the poor woman searched for
her lost coin. Bring him back, dead or alive, within one year,
or don't return to live in this country. I'm confiscating your
lands and all possessions that you have of any value until
you are proven innocent of your apparent guilt by means of
your brother's testimony. [**Duke Frederick** *refers to the
parable in Luke 15:8 in which a poor woman searched her
house for a lost coin, lighting a candle so that she could see
into the dark corners.*]

Oliver   [*trembling with fear*] Oh, I wish Your Highness knew
how I really feel about this! I've never loved my brother in
my life.

Duke Frederick   [*sternly*] Then you're an even worse villain
than I thought.

[*to* **Lords**] Well, throw him out. And tell my officers who
perform such duties to seize his house and lands. Do this
immediately, and send him packing.

[**Duke Frederick**, **Oliver**, *and two or three* **Lords** *all leave.*]

Scene 2

Enter **Orlando** [*with a paper*]

Orlando   Hang there, my verse, in witness of my love,
  And thou, thrice-crowned queen of night, survey
  With thy chaste eye, from thy pale sphere above,
  Thy huntress' name that my full life doth sway.
5 O Rosalind, these trees shall be my books,
  And in their barks my thoughts I'll character,
  That every eye which in this forest looks
  Shall see thy virtue witness'd every where.
  Run, run, Orlando, carve on every tree
10 The fair, the chaste, and unexpressive she.

Exit.

Enter **Corin** *and Clown* [**Touchstone**].

Corin   And how like you this shepherd's life, Master
  Touchstone?

Scene 2

The Forest of Arden.

[**Orlando** *enters, holding a paper in his hand.*]

Orlando   [*He attaches the paper to a tree.*] Hang there, my poem, and tell everyone of my love. And you, goddess of the night, look with your virginal eye from the moon, your pale sphere, upon the name of your huntress Rosalind who rules my entire existence. [*The "thrice-crowned queen of the night" refers to the mythological moon goddess, which had three manifestations: Luna, the moon goddess; Diana, the goddess of chastity; and Proserpina, the goddess of the underworld.*]

[*to the absent* **Rosalind**] Oh, Rosalind! These trees shall be my books, and I'll carve my thoughts in their bark so that everyone who looks in this forest will see the record of your excellence everywhere.

[*to himself*] Run, run, Orlando! Carve on every tree how beautiful, pure, and indescribable she is.

[**Orlando** *runs off.*]

[**Corin** *and* **Touchstone** *enter.*]

Corin   And how do you like living as a shepherd, Mr. Touchstone?

Touchstone   Truly, shepherd, in respect of itself, it is
a good life; but in respect that it is a shepherd's life,
15 it is naught. In respect that it is solitary, I like
it very well; but in respect that it is private, it is a
very vild life. Now in respect it is in the fields, it
pleaseth me well; but in respect it is not in the court,
it is tedious. As it is a spare life (look you) it fits my
20 humor well; but as there is no more plenty in it,
it goes much against my stomach. Hast any philosophy
in thee, shepherd?

Corin   No more but that I know the more one
24 sickens the worse at ease he is; and that he that
wants money, means, and content is without three
good friends; that the property of rain is to wet and
fire to burn; that good pasture makes fat sheep; and
that a great cause of the night is lack of the sun; that
he that hath learn'd no wit by nature, nor art, may
complain of good breeding, or comes of a very dull
31 kindred.

Touchstone   Such a one is a natural philosopher.
Wast ever in court, shepherd?

Corin   No, truly.

35 **Touchstone**   Then thou art damn'd.

Corin   Nay, I hope.

Touchstone   Truly, thou art damn'd, like an ill-roasted
egg, all on one side.

39 **Corin**   For not being at court? Your reason.

Touchstone   To be honest, shepherd, as to the life itself, it's a good life, but considering the fact that it's a shepherd's life, it's bad. As to the fact that it's solitary, I like it very well, but considering the fact that it's lonely, it's a really terrible life. Now, as to being out in the fields, it's very pleasant, but considering the fact that it's not at the court, it's extremely boring. In the sense that it's a simple life, you see, it suits my disposition well, but because it's not a life of abundance, my stomach hates it. Do you like to think philosophically, shepherd? [**Touchstone's** *reference to "stomach" is a play on words, the other meaning being "inclination."*]

Corin   Only to the extent that I know that the sicker someone is, the worse he feels, and that he who lacks money, resources, and contentment is without three good friends. And I know that rain makes things wet and fire makes things burn. I know that good pasture makes well-fed sheep, and that the major cause of nighttime is lack of sunshine, and that the one who isn't smart either by birth or by education will complain about his upbringing or that he comes from a stupid family.

Touchstone   [*impressed in spite of himself*] This man is a natural philosopher! Were you ever at court, shepherd?

Corin   No, indeed.

Touchstone   [*shaking his head in feigned sorrow*] Then you are damned.

Corin   [*shocked*] I hope not.

Touchstone   [**Touchstone's** *comments in this scene are not intended seriously. He is joking with* **Corin,** *and* **Corin** *knows that he is.*] Yes, you are damned like a badly roasted egg, cooked only on one side.

Corin   Because I've never been to court? Explain why you say so.

Touchstone   Why, if thou never wast at court, thou
never saw'st good manners; if thou never saw'st
good manners, then thy manners must be wicked,
and wickedness is sin, and sin is damnation. Thou
44   art in a parlous state, shepherd.

Corin   Not a whit, Touchstone. Those that are
good manners at the court are as ridiculous in the
country as the behavior of the country is most
mockable at the court. You told me you salute
49   not at the court but you kiss your hands; that
courtesy would be uncleanly if courtiers were shepherds.

Touchstone   Instance, briefly; come, instance.

Corin   Why, we are still handling our ewes, and
54   their fells you know are greasy.

Touchstone   Why, do not your courtier's hands sweat?
And is not the grease of a mutton as wholesome as
the sweat of a man? Shallow, shallow. A better
instance, I say; come.

59 **Corin**   Besides, our hands are hard.

Touchstone   Your lips will feel them the sooner.
Shallow again. A more sounder instance, come.

Corin   And they are often tarr'd over with the
surgery of our sheep; and would you have us kiss
64   tar? The courtier's hands are perfum'd with civet.

Touchstone   Why, if you've never been to court, you've never seen good manners; if you've never seen good manners, then your manners must be bad, and being bad is sin, and sin results in being damned. You're in great danger, shepherd. [*"Manners" could refer to either deportment or morals.*]

Corin   Not at all, Touchstone. The good manners of the court are as ridiculous in the country as the behavior of the country is absurd at court. You told me that you never fail to kiss one another's hand when you greet people at court; that courteous act would be dirty if those at court were shepherds.

Touchstone   Prove it quickly. Come, prove it.

Corin   Why, because we are constantly handling our ewes, and their fleeces, you know, are greasy.

Touchstone   Why, don't the hands of courtiers sweat? And isn't the grease of a sheep just as wholesome as the sweat of a man? Your reasoning isn't deep enough. I want better proof, I tell you. Come on.

Corin   Also, our hands are rough.

Touchstone   Then your lips will feel them even sooner. That's still not proof. Give me an even stronger reason. Come on.

Corin   [*triumphantly, after giving the matter some thought*] And shepherds' hands are often covered with the tar used on the cuts on the sheep's skin. Would you have us kiss tar? Courtiers' hands are perfumed with civet.

Touchstone   Most shallow man! thou worm's-meat,
in respect of a good piece of flesh indeed! Learn
of the wise, and perpend: civet is of a baser birth
than tar, the very uncleanly flux of a cat. Mend
69   the instance, shepherd.

Corin   You have too courtly a wit for me, I'll rest.

Touchstone   Wilt thou rest damn'd? God help thee,
shallow man! God make incision in thee, thou art raw.

Corin   Sir, I am a true laborer: I earn that I eat,
74   get that I wear, owe no man hate, envy no man's
happiness, glad of other men's good, content with my
harm, and the greatest of my pride is to see my ewes
graze and my lambs suck.

Touchstone   That is another simple sin in you, to bring
79   the ewes and the rams together and to offer to get
your living by the copulation of cattle; to be bawd to a
bell-wether, and to betray a she-lamb of a twelvemonth to a crooked-pated old cuckoldly ram, out of
83   all reasonable match. If thou beest not damn'd
for this, the devil himself will have no shepherds;
I cannot see else how thou shouldst scape.

Corin   Here comes young Master Ganymed, my
new mistress's brother.

Enter **Rosalind** [*with a paper, reading*].

Touchstone   You shallow thinker! You're no more a thinker than meat infested with maggots is a good steak! Learn from the wise and think about what I'm about to say. Civet is even less clean than tar because it's the filthy secretion of a cat. Repair your proof, shepherd.

Corin   [*shaking his head good-naturedly*] Your wit is too courtly for me. I give up.

Touchstone   [*pretending to be shocked*] Are you willing to give up while you are damned? God help you, shallow thinker! May God make an incision in you; you are ill. [**Touchstone** *refers to the practice of draining "bad" blood.*]

Corin   Sir, I'm an honest laborer: I earn what I eat and buy what I wear, I hate no one, envy no one's happiness, am glad about other people's good luck and resigned when I have bad luck, and my greatest pride is watching my ewes graze and my lambs suckle.

Touchstone   That's another of your bold-faced sins; you make your living by bringing ewes and rams together to have sex! You're a pimp for a male sheep, forcing a young female lamb to mate with a crooked-horned, foolish old ram, a completely incompatible match. If you don't go to hell for this, the devil himself is refusing to let shepherds in; I can't see how else you could avoid it.

Corin   Here comes young Master Ganymede, my new mistress's brother.

[**Rosalind**, *dressed as* **Ganymede** *enters, reading a sheet of paper.*]

[**Rosalind**]   "From the east to western Inde,
No jewel is like Rosalind.
90   Her worth, being mounted on the wind,
Through all the world bears Rosalind.
All the pictures fairest lin'd
Are but black to Rosalind.
Let no face be kept in mind
95   But the fair of Rosalind."

Touchstone   I'll rhyme you so eight years together,
dinners and suppers and sleeping-hours excepted.
It is the right butter-women's rank to market.

Rosalind   Out, fool!

100 **Touchstone**   For a taste:
If a hart do lack a hind,
Let him seek out Rosalind.
If the cat will after kind,
So be sure will Rosalind.
105   Wint'red garments must be lin'd,
So must slender Rosalind.
They that reap must sheaf and bind,
Then to cart with Rosalind.
Sweetest nut hath sourest rind,
110   Such a nut is Rosalind.
He that sweetest rose will find,
Must find love's prick and Rosalind.
This is the very false gallop of verses; why do you
114   infect yourself with them?

Rosalind   [as **Ganymede**, reading aloud]
      "From the East to the Western Ind,
      There's no jewel like Rosalind.
      Throughout the world, carried on the wind,
      Is the worth of Rosalind.
      The most beautiful pictures drawn
      Are black compared to Rosalind.
      Imagine no beauty in your mind
      But that of lovely Rosalind."

[The "east and western Ind" refers to India and the islands of
the Malay archipelago. "Black" meant "ugly" and was the
opposite of "fair," which meant "beautiful"; Elizabethans
considered blondes to be the most attractive women.]

Touchstone   I'll write you poetry like that for the next eight
years, nonstop except when I'm eating dinner or supper, or
when I'm asleep. It plods along like dairy-women marching
to market.

Rosalind   [still poring over the poem] Quiet, fool!

Touchstone   [with twinkling eyes] I'll give you a free sample:
      If a buck should lack a hind
      Let him look for Rosalind.
      If a cat is sure to mate,
      Lust is Rosalind's certain fate.
      A winter coat, stuffed, is "lined,"
      And so is slender Rosalind.
      The reapers must the wheat sheaves bind
      And put on a cart, like Rosalind.
      The sweetest nut has the sourest rind,
      And that is just like Rosalind.
      The sweetest rose you'll ever find
      Is full of thorns—like Rosalind.

This is how bad poetry limps along. Why are you contami-
nating yourself with it?

Rosalind   Peace, you dull fool, I found them on a tree.

Touchstone   Truly, the tree yields bad fruit.

Rosalind   I'll graff it with you, and then I shall graff
118   it with a medlar. Then it will be the earliest
fruit i' th' country; for you'll be rotten ere you be
half ripe, and that's the right virtue of the medlar.

Touchstone   You have said; but whether wisely or no,
let the forest judge.

Enter **Celia** *with a writing.*

Rosalind   Peace,
Here comes my sister reading, stand aside.

[*A "hind" is a female deer. "Lined" referred to the copulation (that is, the sexual activity) of dogs. Also,* **Touchstone's** *mention of a cart refers to the practice of exposing prostitutes and shrewish women to public ridicule by driving them through the streets in a cart.*]

Rosalind [*amused but somewhat impatient*] Hush, you stupid fool! I found the poem hanging on a tree.

Touchstone [*shaking his head with feigned regret*] Indeed, the tree has bad fruit. [*He refers to Matthew 7:18, which says, "A good tree cannot bring forth evil fruit, neither can a corrupt tree bring forth good fruit."*]

Rosalind I'll graft you to the tree, and then I'll be grafting it with a medlar. Then it will be the fruit that ripens soonest in the country because you will be rotten before you're even half-ripe, like a medlar. [*The medlar is a fruit that is not edible until it is rotten. Because* **Touchstone** *has meddled with her while she was reading her poem,* **Rosalind** *puns on the word "meddler," implying that* **Touchstone**, *like the fruit, is rotten.*]

Touchstone You have spoken, but we'll let the forest decide whether or not you have spoken wisely.

[**Celia** *enters, with a piece of paper.*]

Rosalind Be quiet! Here comes my cousin, reading something. Let's stand to the side.

Celia   [*Reads.*]
125   "Why should this [a] desert be?
            For it is unpeopled? No!
        Tongues I'll hang on every tree,
            That shall civil sayings show:
        Some, how brief the life of man
130   Runs his erring pilgrimage,
        That the stretching of a span
            Buckles in his sum of age;
        Some, of violated vows
            'Twixt the souls of friend and friend;
135   But upon the fairest boughs,
            Or at every sentence end,
        Will I 'Rosalinda' write,
            Teaching all that read to know
        The quintessence of every sprite
140   Heaven would in little show.
        Therefore heaven Nature charg'd
            That one body should be fill'd
        With all graces wide-enlarg'd.
            Nature presently distill'd
145   Helen's cheek, but not [her] heart,
            Cleopatra's majesty,
        Atalanta's better part,
            Sad Lucretia's modesty.
        Thus Rosalind of many parts
150   By heavenly synod was devis'd,
        Of many faces, eyes, and hearts,
            To have the touches dearest priz'd.
        Heaven would that she these gifts should have,
154   And I to live and die her slave."

Celia   [*dressed as* **Aliena** *reading aloud with amusement*]
Should this place be deserted
Because no one lives here? No.
I'll give tongues to every tree
So that, in these poems, the trees may speak cleverly.
Some will tell how short man's life is
As he blunders along on his journey;
It's as short as the distance
Between your thumb and little finger.
Some will tell of broken promises
Between the souls of friends.
But on the loveliest branches
Or with clever sayings,
I will write of Rosalind,
Teaching everyone who reads these poems
That highest perfection of human spirit
That Heaven has revealed in her.
Therefore, Heaven ordered Nature
To put within Rosalind's being
Every possible virtue found in women everywhere.
She has the beauty of Helen of Troy, but not her
    unfaithful heart.
She has Cleopatra's royal bearing,
Atalanta's best quality,
And sad Lucretia's modesty.
So, by a committee of gods,
Rosalind was designed
To have the very best features
Of all faces, eyes, and hearts.
Heaven chose that she should have these gifts
And that I should live and die as her slave.

[*Helen of Troy and Cleopatra, the queen of Egypt, were both
    famed for their beauty. In mythology, Atalanta was famed
    for her chastity, as was Lucretia, who committed suicide
    after being raped by King Tarquin.*]

139

Rosalind   O most gentle Jupiter, what tedious homily
of love have you wearied your parishioners withal,
and never cried, "Have patience, good people!"

Celia   How now? back, friends! Shepherd, go off a
159   little. Go with him, sirrah.

Touchstone   Come, shepherd, let us make an honorable
retreat, though not with bag and baggage, yet with
scrip and scrippage.

Exit [*with* **Corin**].

Celia   Didst thou hear these verses?

Rosalind   O yes, I heard them all, and more too,
for some of them had in them more feet than the
166   verses would bear.

Celia   That's no matter; the feet might bear the
verses.

Rosalind   Ay, but the feet were lame, and could not
bear themselves without the verse, and therefore stood
171   lamely in the verse.

Celia   But didst thou hear without wondering how
thy name should be hang'd and carv'd upon these trees?

Rosalind   [*coming forward, speaking jokingly as* **Ganymede**]
Oh, gentle preacher! Have you tired out your congregation
with this boring sermon on love, yet not begged them,
"Be patient, good people"?

Celia   [*as* **Aliena**, *exclaiming in mock indignation, seeing
that she has been spied upon by* **Rosalind**, **Touchstone**,
and **Corin**] What? Traitors!

[*to* **Corin**] Shepherd, walk off a short distance.

[*to* **Touchstone**] Go with him, fellow.

Touchstone   Come, shepherd. Let's make an honorable
retreat; although we don't leave with military equipment,
we have our shepherd's pouches and what's inside them.
[*That is, like an army making an orderly retreat, they carry
all their equipment with them.*]

[**Touchstone** *and* **Corin** *leave.*]

Celia   [*shaking her head in mock dismay*] Did you hear these
poems?

Rosalind   [joking to hide her pleasure at **Orlando's** devo-
tion] Oh, yes, I heard them all, and more, too. Some of
them had more feet in them than the lines could carry. [*She
refers to the number of poetic beats or "feet" in the poem,
saying that the writer has crammed too many beats into the
lines of the poem.*]

Celia   That's no problem; the feet should carry the lines.

Rosalind   Yes, but the feet were lame and couldn't support
the lines without the help of the verse, so they stood lamely
in the verse.

Celia   But did you hear them without wondering how your
name came to be hung and carved on these trees?

141

Rosalind   I was seven of the nine days out of the wonder
before you came; for look here what I found on a palm
176   tree. I was never so berhym'd since Pythagoras'
time, that I was an Irish rat, which I can hardly
remember.

Celia   Trow you who hath done this?

180   **Rosalind**   Is it a man?

Celia   And a chain, that you once wore, about his
neck. Change you color?

Rosalind   I prithee, who?

Celia   O Lord, Lord, it is a hard matter for friends
to meet; but mountains may be remov'd with earth-
186   quakes, and so encounter.

Rosalind   Nay, but who is it?

Celia   Is it possible?

Rosalind   Nay, I prithee now, with most petitionary
190   vehemence, tell me who it is.

Celia   O wonderful, wonderful, and most wonderful
wonderful! and yet again wonderful, and after that,
out of all hooping!

Rosalind   I had already been exposed to most of this "nine days wonder" before you got here. Look at what I found on a palm tree. I haven't been so attacked with rhymes since I was an Irish rat in Pythagoras' time—which I can hardly remember. [*The Irish, according to legend, could kill rats by uttering rhyming incantations. Pythagoras taught that souls migrated from humans to animals.*]

Celia   Can you guess who has done this?

Rosalind   Is it a man?

Celia   [*teasingly*] With a chain, that you once wore, around his neck. Are you blushing?

Rosalind   Please, who is it?

Celia   [*clapping her hands and laughing delightedly*] Oh, Lord, Lord! It's hard for friends to find one another, but earthquakes can move mountains so that they do so. [**Celia** *alters a proverb that says, "Friends may meet, but mountains never greet."*]

Rosalind   No, but who is it?

Celia   Are you serious?

Rosalind   [*afraid to believe that the answer could be what she hopes it to be*] No, now please, I earnestly beg of you. Tell me who it is.

Celia   Oh, it's wonderful, wonderful, most wonderfully wonderful, and even more wonderful, and beyond-words wonderful!

Rosalind   Good my complexion, dost thou think,
though I am caparison'd like a man, I have a doublet
and hose in my disposition? One inch of delay more is
197   a South-sea of discovery. I prithee tell me who is
it quickly, and speak apace. I would thou couldst
stammer, that thou mightst pour this conceal'd man
out of thy mouth, as wine comes out of a narrow-
mouth'd bottle, either too much at once, or none at all.
I prithee take the cork out of thy mouth that I may
203   drink thy tidings.

Celia   So you may put a man in your belly.

Rosalind   Is he of God's making? What manner of
man? Is his head worth a hat? or his chin worth a
207   beard?

Celia   Nay, he hath but a little beard.

Rosalind   Why, God will send more, if the man will
be thankful. Let me stay the growth of his beard, if
211   thou delay me not the knowledge of his chin.

Celia   It is young Orlando, that tripp'd up the
wrastler's heels, and your heart, both in an instant.

Rosalind   Nay, but the devil take mocking. Speak sad
215   brow and true maid.

Celia   I' faith, coz, 'tis he.

Rosalind   Orlando?

Celia   Orlando.

Rosalind   Have mercy on my feminine curiosity! Do you think that, just because I'm dressed as a man, I wear a man's clothing within my heart? One inch more of delay is as endless as a voyage of exploration to the South Pacific Ocean. I beg you to tell me quickly who it is—and speak fast. I wish you could stutter so that you could pour this mystery man out of your mouth the way wine comes out of a narrow-mouthed bottle, either too much at once or none at all. I beg you to take the cork out of your mouth so that I may drink your news.

Celia   So that you may put a man in your belly. [*She jokingly refers to* **Rosalind's** *physical desire for* **Orlando**, *which could result in* **Rosalind's** *conceiving a male child by him.*]

Rosalind   Is he a normal human being? What's he like? Is his head worth putting a hat on or his chin deserving of a beard? [*The expression "of God's own making" was a proverbial saying meaning "a normal human being."*]

Celia   No, he only has a little beard.

Rosalind   Well, God will send him more whiskers if he will be thankful for them. I'm willing to wait for his beard to fill out if you don't put off telling me who that chin belongs to.

Celia   It's young Orlando, the man who overthrew both the wrestler and your heart at the same moment.

Rosalind   [*gasping with delight mixed with fear*] No! If you're joking, may the devil get you! Tell me, in seriousness and honesty.

Celia   [*holding up her hand as if taking an oath*] I swear, cousin, it is he.

Rosalind   [*not daring to believe*] Orlando?

Celia   [*nodding emphatically*] Orlando.

Rosalind   Alas the day, what shall I do with my doublet
220   and hose? What did he when thou saw'st him?
What said he? How look'd he? Wherein went he?
What makes him here? Did he ask for me? Where
remains he? How parted he with thee? And when
shalt thou see him again? Answer me in one word.

Celia   You must borrow me Gargantua's mouth
226   first; 'tis a word too great for any mouth of this
age's size. To say ay and no to these particulars is
more than to answer in a catechism.

Rosalind   But doth he know that I am in this forest
and in man's apparel? Looks he as freshly as he did
231   the day he wrastled?

Celia   It is as easy to count atomies as to resolve the
propositions of a lover. But take a taste of my finding
him, and relish it with good observance. I found him
235   under a tree, like a dropp'd acorn.

Rosalind   It may well be call'd Jove's tree, when it
drops [such] fruit.

Celia   Give me audience, good madam.

Rosalind   Proceed.

Celia   There lay he, stretch'd along, like a wounded
241   knight.

Rosalind   [*at first, in dismay over her predicament, but then she eagerly questions* **Celia**] Oh, no! What am I going to do about my man's jacket and trousers? What did he do when you saw him? What did he say? How did he look? How was he dressed? What is he doing here? Did he ask for me? Where is he living? How did he say goodbye to you? And when will you see him again? Answer me in a word. [*"In a word" means "quickly," but* **Celia**, *in her next lines, pretends to take* **Rosalind** *literally.*]

Celia   You must lend me Gargantua's mouth first! It would take a bigger word than anyone's mouth today could accommodate. To just answer "yes" or "no" to all these questions would be worse than answering questions in a catechism. [*Gargantua, according to Rabelais' version of the folk tale, was a giant who swallowed five pilgrims in a salad. A catechism is a set of questions and answers pertaining to religious doctrine.*]

Rosalind   But does he know that I'm in this forest and wearing men's clothing? Does he look as vigorous as he did the day he wrestled?

Celia   [*shaking her head in mock disgust*] It's as easy to count dust specks in a beam of sunlight as it is to answer the questions of a lover. But taste how I found him, and savor it by paying close attention. I found him lying under a tree like a dropped acorn.

Rosalind   [*to herself*] It should be called "God's tree" if it drops such fine fruit. [*The oak tree was sacred to Jove, also called "Jupiter."*]

Celia   [*with mock sternness*] Pay attention, good lady.

Rosalind   Go on.

Celia   [*in an overly dramatic tone*] There he lay, stretched out full length like a wounded knight.

Rosalind   Though it be pity to see such a sight, it well becomes the ground.

Celia   Cry "holla" to [thy] tongue, I prithee; it curvets unseasonably. He was furnish'd like a hunter.

246 **Rosalind**   O ominous! he comes to kill my heart.

Celia   I would sing my song without a burthen; thou bring'st me out of tune.

Rosalind   Do you not know I am a woman? when
250   I think, I must speak. Sweet, say on.

Enter **Orlando** *and* **Jaques**.

Celia   You bring me out. Soft, comes he not here?

Rosalind   'Tis he. Slink by, and note him.

Jaques   I thank you for your company, but, good faith, I had as lief have been myself alone.

Orlando   And so had I; but yet for fashion sake I
256   thank you too for your society.

Jaques   God buy you, let's meet as little as we can.

Orlando   I do desire we may be better strangers.

Jaques   I pray you mar no more trees with writing
260   love-songs in their barks.

Rosalind   Although it would be a sad sight, it would make the ground look attractive.

Celia   Cry "Whoa!" to your tongue, please! It's prancing about like an out-of-control horse when it shouldn't be. He was dressed like a hunter.

Rosalind   That's ominous! He has come to kill my heart. [*She puns on "heart" and "hart," another word for a deer.*]

Celia   I would like to sing my song without your "harmony"; you're making me sing off-key.

Rosalind   Have you forgotten that I'm a woman? When I think something, I have to say it. Go ahead, Sweetie.

[**Orlando** *and* **Jaques** *enter.*]

Celia   [*querulously*] You're confusing me.

[*suddenly noticing the entrance of* **Orlando** *and* **Jaques**] Wait, isn't that him coming this way?

Rosalind   It is! Let's sneak away and watch what he does.

[**Rosalind** *and* **Celia** *hide themselves.*]

Jaques   Thank you for your company, but to be honest I would rather have been alone.

Orlando   So would I. But, just to be polite, I will thank you for your company, too.

Jaques   [*cordially*] Goodbye. Let's meet as seldom as we can.

Orlando   [*with equal cordiality*] I hope that we may be like strangers.

Jaques   I beg you not to disfigure any more trees by carving love-poems in their bark.

Orlando   I pray you mar no moe of my verses with reading them ill-favoredly.

Jaques   Rosalind is your love's name?

Orlando   Yes, just.

265 **Jaques**   I do not like her name.

Orlando   There was no thought of pleasing you when she was christen'd.

Jaques   What stature is she of?

269 **Orlando**   Just as high as my heart.

Jaques   You are full of pretty answers; have you not been acquainted with goldsmiths' wives, and conn'd them out of rings?

Orlando   Not so; but I answer you right painted cloth, from whence you have studied your ques-
275   tions.

Jaques   You have a nimble wit; I think 'twas made of Atalanta's heels. Will you sit down with me? and we two will rail against our mistress the world, and all our misery.

Orlando   I will chide no breather in the world but my-
281   self, against whom I know most faults.

Jaques   The worst fault you have is to be in love.

Orlando   'Tis a fault I will not change for your best virtue. I am weary of you.

Orlando   I beg you not to disfigure any more of my poems by reading them badly.

Jaques   Is your love's name "Rosalind"?

Orlando   Yes, that's right.

Jaques   [*shaking his head regretfully*] I don't like her name.

Orlando   No one was worried about pleasing you when she was christened.

Jaques   How tall is she?

Orlando   Just as tall as my heart.

Jaques   [*with mock approval*] You're full of clever answers. Have you known goldsmiths' wives and memorized the sayings that are engraved inside rings?

Orlando   No, but I can answer you correctly from the clichés on cheap wall hangings from which you learned your questions.

Jaques   You have a quick wit. I think it was made out of Atalanta's heels. Will you sit down with me? And we two will complain about our mistress—the world, that is—and all our problems. [*Atalanta, according to mythology, was able to outrun all her suitors. She was finally beaten by Hippomenes, who dropped three golden apples that Atalanta paused to pick up and thus was outrun.*]

Orlando   I will criticize no living person in the world except myself because I know my many faults.

Jaques   The worst fault you have is being in love.

Orlando   It's a fault I wouldn't trade for your best quality. I'm tired of you.

Jaques   By my troth, I was seeking for a fool when I
286   found you.

Orlando   He is drown'd in the brook; look but in,
and you shall see him.

Jaques   There I shall see mine own figure.

Orlando   Which I take to be either a fool or a cipher.

Jaques   I'll tarry no longer with you. Farewell, good
292   Signior Love.

Orlando   I am glad of your departure. Adieu, good
Monsieur Melancholy.

[*Exit* **Jaques.**]

Rosalind   [*Aside to* **Celia.**] I will speak to him like a
saucy lackey, and under that habit play the knave
297   with him.—Do you hear, forester?

Orlando   Very well. What would you?

Rosalind   I pray you, what is't a' clock?

Orlando   You should ask me what time o' day; there's
301   no clock in the forest.

Rosalind   Then there is no true lover in the forest,
else sighing every minute and groaning every hour
would detect the lazy foot of Time as well as a
305   clock.

Jaques   I swear to you that I was looking for a fool when I found you. [*He is referring to* **Touchstone**, *but he implies that he found a different sort of fool in* **Orlando**.]

Orlando   He is drowned in the brook. If you look in, you will see him. [*He means that, by seeing his own reflection,* **Jaques** *will see a fool.*]

Jaques   I'll see myself there.

Orlando   Which would be either a fool or a nobody.

Jaques   I'll waste no more time with you. Goodbye, good Signior Love. [*"Signior" means "mister" in Italian.*]

Orlando   I'm glad you're leaving. Adieu, good Monsieur Melancholy. [*"Adieu" is French for "goodbye."*]

[**Jaques** *leaves.*]

Rosalind   [*softly, to* **Celia**] I'll talk to him as if I'm a disrespectful servant, and in that role, deceive him. [**Rosalind's** *words "play the knave" meant not only to pretend that she is a boy but also to trick someone in a game.*]

[*as* **Ganymede**, *raising her voice to speak to* **Orlando**] Can you hear me, forester?

Orlando   Very well. What do you want?

Rosalind   What hour is it, please? [*Momentarily flustered at speaking to her beloved at last,* **Rosalind** *blurts out a foolish question.*]

Orlando   [*giving* **Ganymede** *a searching look because of the odd question*] You should ask me what time of day it is; there are no clocks in the forest.

Rosalind   [*quickly recovering her composure*] Then there are no genuine lovers in the forest either; otherwise, their sighing every minute and groaning every hour would reveal the slow foot of Time passing just as well as a clock would.

Orlando   And why not the swift foot of Time? Had not that been as proper?

Rosalind   By no means, sir. Time travels in divers paces with divers persons. I'll tell you who Time ambles withal, who Time trots withal, who Time
311   gallops withal, and who he stands still withal.

Orlando   I prithee, who doth he trot withal?

Rosalind   Marry, he trots hard with a young maid between the contract of her marriage and the day it is solemniz'd. If the interim be but a se'nnight, Time's pace is so hard that it seems the length of
317   seven year.

Orlando   Who ambles Time withal?

Rosalind   With a priest that lacks Latin, and a rich man that hath not the gout; for the one sleeps easily because he cannot study, and the other lives mer-
322   rily because he feels no pain; the one lacking the burthen of lean and wasteful learning, the other knowing no burthen of heavy tedious penury. These
325   Time ambles withal.

Orlando   Who doth he gallop withal?

Rosalind   With a thief to the gallows; for though he go as softly as foot can fall, he thinks himself too soon there.

Orlando Why wouldn't it be the swift foot of Time? Wouldn't that be just as accurate?

Rosalind Not at all, sir. Time travels at different speeds for different people. I'll tell you who Time ambles along for, who Time trots for, who Time gallops for, and who it stands still for. [**Rosalind** *refers to the paces of a horse, ambling being the slowest, trotting being a moderate speed, and galloping being the fastest.*]

Orlando Please, tell me, who does Time trot for?

Rosalind Indeed, it trots at an uncomfortable pace for the young maiden between the day of her engagement to the day when she is actually married; even if the time between is only seven days, Time trots so hard that it seems like seven years. [**Rosalind**, *in saying that Time trots "hard" means that the pace is so uncomfortable for the rider that it makes the ride seem long.*]

Orlando [*amused and intrigued*] Who does Time amble for?

Rosalind For the priest who can't read Latin and a rich man who doesn't have the gout; the first one sleeps well, because he doesn't have to study, and the other lives happily because he isn't in pain. One isn't burdened by unprofitable study that makes him waste away, and the other doesn't know the burden of dreadful and wearying poverty. Time ambles for these people. [*An uneducated priest, also called a "hedge priest," wouldn't be able to study because at that time the Bible and other theological texts were available only in Latin.*]

Orlando Who does it gallop for?

Rosalind For the thief going to the gallows, because even though he may walk as slowly as his feet can go, he gets there too soon.

330 **Orlando** Who stays it still withal?

Rosalind With lawyers in the vacation; for they sleep between term and term, and then they perceive not how Time moves.

334 **Orlando** Where dwell you, pretty youth?

Rosalind With this shepherdess, my sister; here in the skirts of the forest, like fringe upon a petti-coat.

Orlando Are you native of this place?

Rosalind As the cony that you see dwell where she is
340   kindled.

Orlando Your accent is something finer than you could purchase in so remov'd a dwelling.

Rosalind I have been told so of many; but indeed an old religious uncle of mine taught me to speak, who was in his youth an inland man, one that knew courtship too well, for there he fell in love. I have
347   heard him read many lectures against it, and I thank God I am not a woman, to be touch'd with so many giddy offences as he hath generally tax'd
350   their whole sex withal.

Orlando Can you remember any of the principal evils that he laid to the charge of women?

Orlando   Who does it stand still for?

Rosalind   For lawyers on vacation, because they sleep away the interval between judicial sessions, and therefore they don't realize that time is passing.

Orlando   Where do you live, pretty young man?

Rosalind   [*indicating* **Celia**, *dressed as* **Aliena**] With this shepherdess, my sister. We live here on the forest's out-skirts, like the fringe on a petticoat.

Orlando   Were you born in this place?

Rosalind   [*nodding in the affirmative*] Just like the rabbit that lives where she is born.

Orlando   You speak in a more refined way than you could have acquired in so remote a place as this. [*Because poor people could not afford to hire tutors for their children, typically their way of speaking was noticeably different from that of those who were educated.*]

Rosalind   [*searching quickly for a reasonable excuse*] Many people have told me that. But, in fact, an old uncle of mine who was part of a religious order taught me to speak; he was raised in the city. He knew all too well about courtship, for while at court he fell in love. I've often heard him warn against love, and I thank God that I'm not a woman, infected with all the foolish flaws as he has accused the whole sex of having.

Orlando   Can you remember any of the primary evils that he charged women with?

Rosalind   There were none principal, they were all
like one another as halfpence are, every one fault
seeming monstrous till his fellow-fault came to
356   match it.

Orlando   I prithee recount some of them.

Rosalind   No; I will not cast away my physic but
on those that are sick. There is a man haunts the
forest, that abuses our young plants with carving "Rosalind" on their barks; hangs odes upon haw-
362   thorns, and elegies on brambles; all, forsooth,
[deifying] the name of Rosalind. If I could meet that
fancy-monger, I would give him some good counsel,
for he seems to have the quotidian of love upon
366   him.

Orlando   I am he that is so love-shak'd, I pray you
tell me your remedy.

Rosalind   There is none of my uncle's marks upon you.
He taught me how to know a man in love; in which
371   cage of rushes I am sure you [are] not prisoner.

Orlando   What were his marks?

Rosalind   There weren't any that were primary. They were all as similar to one another as halfpence are, every fault seeming monstrous until the next fault came along, which was just as bad. [*Halfpence, coins worth a half-cent, had identical markings.*]

Orlando   [*still amused*] Please, tell me some of them.

Rosalind   [*pretending that she doesn't know that she is speaking to the man to whom she refers*] No, I won't throw away my medicine; I'll give it only to those who are sick. There's a man haunting the forest who abuses the young trees by carving "Rosalind" on their bark; he hangs odes on hawthorns and love poems on blackberry bushes, all of them, I swear, praising the name of Rosalind. If I could find that peddler of love, I would give him some good advice, for he seems to have a love-fever that attacks him every day.

Orlando   I am the man who is so sick with love. Please tell me your cure.

Rosalind   [*looking intently into **Orlando's** face and then shaking her head*] You don't show any of the symptoms of love my uncle told me about. He taught me how to recognize a man in love, and I'm sure you aren't trapped in any such flimsy prison. [*The stalks of the rush plant were used to make baskets; thus, a cage of rushes would be one from which it would not be difficult to escape.*]

Orlando   What did he say the symptoms were?

Rosalind   A lean cheek, which you have not; a blue
eye and sunken, which you have not; an unquestion-
able spirit, which you have not; a beard neglected,
376   which you have not (but I pardon you for that,
for simply your having in beard is a younger brother's revenue); then your hose should be ungarter'd,
your bonnet unbanded, your sleeve unbutton'd,
your shoe untied, and every thing about you dem-
381   onstrating a careless desolation. But you are
no such man; you are rather point-device in your
accoustrements, as loving yourself, than seeming the
lover of any other.

Orlando   Fair youth, I would I could make thee be-
386   lieve I love.

Rosalind   Me believe it? You may as soon make her
that you love believe it, which I warrant she is
apter to do than to confess she does. That is one
of the points in the which women still give the lie
391   to their consciences. But in good sooth, are
you he that hangs the verses on the trees, wherein
Rosalind is so admir'd?

Orlando   I swear to thee, youth, by the white hand of
395   Rosalind, I am that he, that unfortunate he.

Rosalind   But are you so much in love as your rhymes
speak?

Orlando   Neither rhyme nor reason can express how
399   much.

Rosalind A thin face, which you don't have; eyes with dark circles under them, which you don't have; an unsociable personality, which you don't have; an untidy beard, which you don't have—but I excuse you from that one since your beard is actually as scanty as a younger brother's income. Also, you would have forgotten to properly secure your stockings, your hat would not have a fancy band, your sleeve would be unbuttoned, your shoe untied, and every-thing about your appearance would demonstrate that you're too miserable to care how you look. But you're no such man. Instead, you're meticulously neat in your cloth-ing, making it look more like you're in love with yourself than with anyone else.

Orlando [*taking "***Ganymede's***" comments in stride*] Handsome youth, I wish I could make you believe that I'm in love.

Rosalind Make *me* believe it? You have as good a chance of making your sweetheart believe it—which, I would swear, she is more likely to actually do than to admit that she does. That's one of the ways in which women always lie to themselves about their true feelings. But, tell the truth; are you the one who is hanging the poems in which Rosalind is so praised on the trees?

Orlando I swear to you, young man, by Rosalind's white hand that I am the unfortunate man.

Rosalind [*feigning indifference to* **Orlando's** *answer*] But are you as much in love as your poems say?

Orlando Neither poetry nor logic can express how much I love her.

Rosalind   Love is merely a madness, and I tell you,
deserves as well a dark house and a whip as madmen
do; and the reason why they are not so punish'd and
cur'd is, that the lunacy is so ordinary that the
whippers are in love too. Yet I profess curing it
405   by counsel.

Orlando   Did you ever cure any so?

Rosalind   Yes, one, and in this manner. He was to
imagine me his love, his mistress; and I set him
every day to woo me. At which time would I, being
410   but a moonish youth, grieve, be effeminate,
changeable, longing and liking, proud, fantastical,
apish, shallow, inconstant, full of tears, full of smiles;
for every passion something, and for no passion
truly any thing, as boys and women are for the
415   most part cattle of this color; would now like
him, now loathe him; then entertain him, then forswear
him; now weep for him, then spit at him; that I
drave my suitor from his mad humor of love to a
419   living humor of madness, which was, to forswear
the full stream of the world, and to live in a nook
merely monastic. And thus I cur'd him, and this
way will I take upon me to wash your liver as clean
as a sound sheep's heart, that there shall not be one
spot of love in't.

425 **Orlando**   I would not be cur'd, youth.

Rosalind   I would cure you, if you would but call me
Rosalind, and come every day to my cote and woo me.

Orlando   Now, by the faith of my love, I will. Tell
429   me where it is.

Rosalind   Love is total insanity, and, I'm telling you, lovers are just as deserving of being locked up in a dark room and whipped as madmen are. The reason lovers aren't punished and cured is that lovesickness is so commonplace that the whippers are in love, too. However, I am an expert in curing it with my advice. [*In Shakespeare's time, the insane were believed to be possessed by the devil; hence, the treatment described by* **Rosalind**.]

Orlando   [*much intrigued*] Have you ever cured anyone that way?

Rosalind   Yes, one man, and this was how I did it: He had to imagine that I was his beloved, his sweetheart, and I gave him the task of wooing me every day. Then I would, being a changeable young thing, be sad, effeminate, moody, temperamental, proud, and erratic. I put on airs, was shallow and fickle, always crying or laughing, acting as if I felt all kinds of emotions but actually feeling nothing—boys and women are both creatures like this. I would like him one minute and detest him the next; I would welcome him and then I would reject him. I would weep for him, and then I would spit at him. I drove my suitor's love-madness out of him, driving him to another form of insanity, which was to renounce the world and to live as a religious hermit. That's how I cured him, and that's how I will take it upon myself to wash your liver as clean as a healthy sheep's heart, so that there isn't one spot of love in it. [*The liver was believed to be where love resided within a person.*]

Orlando   I don't want to be cured, lad.

Rosalind   I will cure you if you would just call me "Rosalind" and come to my cottage every day to woo me.

Orlando   By my faith in my love, I will do it. Tell me where your cottage is.

Rosalind   Go with me to it, and I'll show it you; and
by the way, you shall tell me where in the forest you
live. Will you go?

Orlando   With all my heart, good youth.

Rosalind   Nay, you must call me Rosalind. Come,
435   sister, will you go?

Exeunt.

Scene 3

Enter Clown [**Touchstone**], **Audrey**; *and* **Jaques**
    [*behind*].

Touchstone   Come apace, good Audrey; I will fetch
up your goats, Audrey. And how, Audrey? am I
the man yet? Doth my simple feature content
you?

Audrey   Your features, Lord warrant us! what fea-
6   tures?

Touchstone   I am here with thee and thy goats as the
most capricious poet, honest Ovid, was among the
Goths.

Rosalind   Come with me to it, and I'll show it to you, and along the way you may tell me where you live in the forest. Will you come?

Orlando   Gladly, good lad.

Rosalind   No, you must call me "Rosalind."

[*to* **Celia**, *as* **Aliena**] Come, sister, will you go with us?

[*They all leave together.*]

Scene 3

The Forest of Arden.

[**Touchstone** *and* **Audrey** *enter, with* **Jaques** *following behind, unobserved.*]

Touchstone   Come quickly, dear Audrey. I'll bring your goats, Audrey. And so, Audrey, am I the man for you? Do you like my plain features?

Audrey   Your features! God help us! What features? [*Audrey, an uneducated woman, doesn't know what* **Touchstone** *means by the word "features."*]

Touchstone   Much like the honorable Ovid, that most inge-nious of poets, I'm here with you and your goats, who lived in exile among the Goths. [*He amuses himself with a play on words, based on the similar pronunciation of "goats" and "Goths," that he knows* **Audrey** *will not understand.*]

Jaques   [*Aside.*] O knowledge ill-inhabited, worse
11   than Jove in a thatch'd house!

Touchstone   When a man's verses cannot be understood, nor a man's good wit seconded with the forward child, understanding, it strikes a man more
dead than a great reckoning in a little room. Truly,
16   I would the gods had made thee poetical.

Audrey   I do not know what "poetical" is. Is it
honest in deed and word? Is it a true thing?

Touchstone   No, truly; for the truest poetry is the
20   most feigning, and lovers are given to poetry;
and what they swear in poetry may be said as lovers
they do feign.

Audrey   Do you wish then that the gods had made
me poetical?

25 **Touchstone**   I do, truly; for thou swear'st to me
thou art honest. Now, if thou wert a poet, I might
have some hope thou didst feign.

28 **Audrey**   Would you not have me honest?

Touchstone   No, truly, unless thou wert hard-favor'd;
for honesty coupled to beauty is to have honey a
sauce to sugar.

Jaques   [*Aside.*] A material fool!

Audrey   Well, I am not fair, and therefore I pray
34   the gods make me honest.

Jaques   [*to himself*] This man's knowledge is living in as lowly a house as Jove was when he stayed in the peasants' cottage. [*In Ovid's* Metamorphoses, *the gods Jove and Mercury were entertained in the cottage of the humble peasants, Philemon and his wife, Baucis, who were unaware of the identity of their visitors.*]

Touchstone   [*shaking his head in amused regret*] When a man's poetry isn't understood and his cleverness doesn't receive even so much encouragement as having a clever child who follows his meaning, it's as bad as being given a huge bill for a little room. Honestly, I wish the gods had made you poetical.

Audrey   I don't know what "poetical" means. Is it being virtuous in what I say and do? Is it being truthful?

Touchstone   Not really, because the best poetry is the most artificial; lovers like to write poetry, so it could be said that what they swear is true in poetry is fake.

Audrey   Yet you still wish that the gods had made me poetical?

Touchstone   Yes, I do, for you swear to me that you're honest. If you were a poet, I could hope that you were only pretending to be. [*"Honest" could mean "sexually pure."* **Touchstone** *implies that he wishes that she weren't, so that he could hope to have sex with her without having to marry her.*]

Audrey   [*completely confused*] So you don't want me to be pure?

Touchstone   No, not unless you were ugly, since chastity combined with beauty is like honey added to sugar. [*That is, it would be too much of a good thing.*]

Jaques   [*to himself*] A fool who makes sense!

Audrey   [*piously*] Well, I'm not pretty, so I pray that the gods will make me chaste.

Touchstone   Truly, and to cast away honesty upon
a foul slut were to put good meat into an unclean
dish.

Audrey   I am not a slut, though I thank the gods
39   I am foul.

Touchstone   Well, prais'd be the gods for thy foulness! sluttishness may come hereafter. But be it
as it may be, I will marry thee; and to that end
I have been with Sir Oliver Martext, the vicar of
the next village, who hath promis'd to meet me in
45   this place of the forest and to couple us.

Jaques   [*Aside.*] I would fain see this meeting.

Audrey   Well, the gods give us joy!

Touchstone   Amen. A man may, if he were of a fearful heart, stagger in this attempt; for here we have
50   no temple but the wood, no assembly but horn-
beasts. But what though? Courage! As horns
are odious, they are necessary. It is said, "Many
a man knows no end of his goods." Right! many
a man has good horns, and knows no end of them.
55   Well, that is the dowry of his wife, 'tis none of
his own getting. Horns? even so. Poor men
alone? No, no, the noblest deer hath them as huge
as the rascal. Is the single man therefore bless'd?
No, as a wall'd town is more worthier than a village,
60   so is the forehead of a married man more honorable than the bare brow of a bachelor; and by how
much defense is better than no skill, by so much is a
horn more precious than to want.

Touchstone   Indeed, wasting chastity on a slut who is ugly is like putting good meat on a dirty dish.

Audrey   [*indignantly, unsure of* **Touchstone's** *meaning, but focusing on the word "slut"*] I'm not a slut, but I thank the gods I'm ugly!

Touchstone   [*amused*] Well, I thank the gods that you're ugly! Maybe sluttishness will come later. But in any case, I'm going to marry you, and for that purpose I have spoken to Sir Oliver Martext, the vicar of the next village, who has promised to meet me here in the forest to marry us.

Jaques   [*to himself*] I would love to see this gathering.

Audrey   Well, may the gods give us happiness!

Touchstone   Amen. If a man had a fearful heart, he might have second thoughts about doing this because we have no church here except the forest, no congregation except the beasts with horns. But, so what! Be courageous, Touchstone! Even though horns are disgusting, they're inevitable. People say, "Many men don't even know how much they own." True. Many men don't know about the horns they have on their own heads. Well, that's his wedding gift from his wife; he doesn't earn them himself. Horns? That's right. Do only poor men have this problem? No, no, the most magnificent deer has ones just as large as those of the runt. Is a single man better off then? No, just as a town with a wall is better than an unprotected village, the forehead of a married man is more respectable than the hornless forehead of a bachelor. In the same way that knowing the art of self-defense is better than being without that skill, it's better to risk being a cuckold than not to get any sex. [**Touchstone's** *reference to "beasts with horns" is an allusion to a "cuckold," that is, a husband with an unfaithful wife, in that such men were often mocked by being forced to wear horns on their heads in a public ceremony of ridicule. He uses deer as a metaphor for men with unfaithful wives.*]

Enter **Sir Oliver Martext**.

Here comes Sir Oliver. Sir Oliver Martext, you
65   are well met. Will you dispatch us here under
this tree, or shall we go with you to your chapel?

Sir Oliver Martext   Is there none here to give the woman?

Touchstone   I will not take her on gift of any man.

Sir Oliver Martext   Truly, she must be given, or the marriage
70   is not lawful.

Jaques   [*Discovering himself.*] Proceed, proceed. I'll
give her.

Touchstone   Good even, good Master What-ye-call't;
74   how do you, sir? You are very well met. God
'ild you for your last company. I am very glad to
see you. Even a toy in hand here, sir. Nay, pray
be cover'd.

Jaques   Will you be married, motley?

Touchstone   As the ox hath his bow, sir, the horse his
80   curb, and the falcon her bells, so man hath his
desires; and as pigeons bill, so wedlock would be
nibbling.

[**Sir Oliver Martext** *enters.*]

Here comes Sir Oliver.

[*to* **Sir Oliver**] Sir Oliver Martext, it's good to see you. Will you marry us here under this tree, or should we go to your chapel with you?

Sir Oliver Martext   Isn't there anyone here to give away the bride?

Touchstone   I refuse to take her from another man. [*Deliberately misinterpreting* **Martext's** *meaning,* **Touchstone** *says that he doesn't want to marry* **Audrey** *if she has had sex with another man.*]

Sir Oliver Martext   [*not understanding* **Touchstone's** *meaning*] Really, she must be given away or the marriage is not legal.

Jaques   [*coming forward*] Go on, go on, I'll give her away.

Touchstone   Good evening, dear Mr. What-you-may-call-it! How are you, sir? May God bless you for your company when we were last together. I'm very glad to see you. We have a little matter to attend to here, sir. No, please put on your hat. [**Touchstone** *calls* **Jaques** *"Mr. What-you-may-call-it" to avoid calling him "jakes," which was an alternate pronunciation of* **"Jaques"** *as well as another word for "toilet."*]

Jaques   So you want to get married, fool?

Touchstone   [*shrugging*] The ox has its bow, the horse has its curb, and the falcon has her bells, and likewise man has his lusts which must be controlled, so, like pigeons stroking beaks together, marriage allows people to make love. [*The bow is the piece of curved wood that attaches the ox to the yoke; the curb is part of a horse's bridle; bells were tied to a falcon's legs to make it easier to find her.*]

Jaques   And will you (being a man of your breeding)
be married under a bush like a beggar? Get you
85   to church, and have a good priest that can tell
you what marriage is. This fellow will but join
you together as they join wainscot; then one of you
will prove a shrunk panel, and like green timber
89   warp, warp.

Touchstone   [*Aside.*] I am not in the mind but I were
better to be married of him than of another, for
he is not like to marry me well; and not being well
married, it will be a good excuse for me hereafter
94   to leave my wife.

Jaques   Go thou with me, and let me counsel thee.

Touchstone   Come, sweet Audrey,
We must be married, or we must live in bawdry.
Farewell, good Master Oliver: not,
              "O sweet Oliver,
100   O brave Oliver,
              Leave me not behind thee;"
       but
              "Wind away,
              Be gone, I say,
105   I will not to wedding with thee."

       [*Exeunt* **Jaques**, **Touchstone**, *and* **Audrey**.]

Sir Oliver Martext   'Tis no matter; ne'er a fantastical knave
of them all shall flout me out of my calling.

Exit.

Jaques   And will you, a man of your background, get
married under a bush like a beggar? Take yourself to church
and have a good priest who can tell you what marriage is
about. This fellow will just slap you together like wood pan-
eling being hung on walls. Then one of you will likely turn
out like an unseasoned panel that will lose its shape and
warp. [*He means that, like warping wood, they would pull
apart; that is, they would be unfaithful.*]

Touchstone   [*to himself*] I'm not sure that I wouldn't be
better off married by him than by someone else because he
isn't likely to marry me properly, and if I'm not properly
married, that would give me a good excuse to leave my
wife later on.

Jaques   Come with me and let me advise you.

Touchstone   Come, sweet Audrey. We must either be
married or we'll live in sin. Farewell, good Sir Oliver. Not—
[*singing*]   *Oh, sweet Oliver,*
                       Oh, handsome Oliver,
                       Don't forsake me, Oliver;

But—

[*singing another song*]

                       Go quickly away,
                       Go way, I say.
                       I'm not going to marry you.

[*The first song* **Touchstone** *sings was a popular song in
which a lovesick girl pleads with her lover; the second song
is probably his own improvisation.*]

[**Jaques**, **Touchstone**, *and* **Audrey** *leave.*]

Sir Oliver Martext   It doesn't matter. The mocking of these
crazy people can't make me give up my profession.

[**Sir Oliver Martext** *leaves.*]

Scene 4

Enter **Rosalind** *and* **Celia.**

Rosalind   Never talk to me, I will weep.

Celia   Do, I prithee, but yet have the grace to
consider that tears do not become a man.

Rosalind   But have I not cause to weep?

Celia   As good cause as one would desire, there-
6   fore weep.

Rosalind   His very hair is of the dissembling color.

Celia   Something browner than Judas's. Marry,
his kisses are Judas's own children.

10 **Rosalind**   I' faith, his hair is of a good color.

Celia   An excellent color. Your chestnut was ever
the only color.

Rosalind   And his kissing is as full of sanctity as the
14   touch of holy bread.

Celia   He hath bought a pair of cast lips of Diana.
A nun of winter's sisterhood kisses not more re-
ligiously, the very ice of chastity is in them.

Scene 4

The Forest of Arden.

[**Rosalind** *and* **Celia** *enter, still dressed as* **Ganymede** *and* **Aliena**.]

Rosalind   [*distraught*] Don't talk to me! I'm going to cry.

Celia   Go ahead, but at least admit that men aren't supposed to cry.

Rosalind   But don't I have good reason to cry?

Celia   As good a reason as anyone could ask for, so go on and cry.

Rosalind   [*bursting into tears*] Even his hair is the same color as a liar's hair! [*According to tradition, Judas Iscariot, the betrayer of Jesus, had red hair or a red beard.*]

Celia   I think his hair is somewhat browner than Judas's was, but his kisses are as false as Judas's. [*Judas betrayed Jesus to the soldiers by kissing him.*]

Rosalind   [*defensively*] No, really, his hair is a good color.

Celia   [*humoring her friend*] It's an excellent color. Chestnut has always been the best color.

Rosalind   And his kisses are as holy as the communion bread.

Celia   [*in amused agreement*] His lips are as virtuous as if he had bought leftover lips that once belonged to Diana. A nun who has taken a cold vow of chastity doesn't kiss with greater purity; they're as chaste as if they're made out of ice. [*The goddess Diana was the Roman goddess of the hunt and virginity.*]

Rosalind   But why did he swear he would come this morning, and comes not?

20 **Celia**   Nay certainly there is no truth in him.

Rosalind   Do you think so?

Celia   Yes, I think he is not a pick-purse nor a horse-stealer, but for his verity in love, I do think him as concave as a cover'd goblet or a worm-eaten
25   nut.

Rosalind   Not true in love?

Celia   Yes, when he is in—but I think he is not in.

Rosalind   You have heard him swear downright he was.

Celia   "Was" is not "is." Besides, the oath of [a] lover is no stronger than the word of a tapster;
32   they are both the confirmer of false reckonings. He attends here in the forest on the Duke your father.

Rosalind   I met the Duke yesterday, and had much question with him. He ask'd me of what parentage
37   I was. I told him of as good as he, so he laugh'd and let me go. But what talk we of fathers, when there is such a man as Orlando?

Rosalind   [*moaning*] But why did he swear he would come this morning and then not come?

Celia   [*still humoring* **Rosalind**] No, he certainly is a complete liar.

Rosalind   [*fearfully*] Do you think so?

Celia   Yes, I think that, although he's not a pickpocket or a horse-stealer, when it comes to his faithfulness in love, his promises are as empty as a goblet with a lid on it or a nut with its insides eaten by a worm. [*A goblet that was not in use (in other words, an empty one) would have a cover on it.*]

Rosalind   He's not a trustworthy lover?

Celia   Yes, when he's really in love, but I don't think he is.

Rosalind   You heard him swear emphatically that he was.

Celia   "Was" isn't the same thing as "is." Besides, when a lover swears something, it's no more trustworthy than the promise of a tavern-keeper; they both swear to things that aren't true. He's staying in the forest with your father, the duke. [**Celia** *compares the way tavern-keepers would pad the bill but swear to its accuracy to the way lovers sometimes make promises they don't intend to keep.*]

Rosalind   I met my father in the forest yesterday and had a long conversation with him. He asked me who my parents were, and I told him that my family was as good as his. So he laughed and let me leave. But why are we talking about fathers when we could be talking about a man like Orlando? [*Because of* **Rosalind's** *disguise as* **Ganymede**, *her father had failed to recognize her.*]

Celia   O, that's a brave man! he writes brave
verses, speaks brave words, swears brave oaths, and
42   breaks them bravely, quite traverse, athwart
the heart of his lover, as a puisne tilter, that spurs
his horse but on one side, breaks his staff like a
noble goose. But all's brave that youth mounts and
46   folly guides. Who comes here?

Enter **Corin**.

Corin   Mistress and master, you have oft inquired
After the shepherd that complain'd of love,
Who you saw sitting by me on the turf,
50   Praising the proud disdainful shepherdess
That was his mistress.

Celia   Well; and what of him?

Corin   If you will see a pageant truly play'd
Between the pale complexion of true love
And the red glow of scorn and proud disdain,
55   Go hence a little, and I shall conduct you,
If you will mark it.

Rosalind   O, come, let us remove,
The sight of lovers feedeth those in love.
Bring us to this sight, and you shall say
I'll prove a busy actor in their play.

Exeunt.

Celia [*sarcastically*] Oh, he's a brave man! He writes brave poems, says brave things, swears brave vows and breaks them, along with his beloved's heart, without a second thought. He's like a bad jouster who spurs his horse so poorly that it doesn't even run straight, and he breaks his lance in trying to cheat, like the complete fool that he is. But everything seems fine when you're a young person being led by your own foolishness. [*The word "brave" as* **Celia** *uses it means "excellent," but she ironically contrasts the two meanings of "brave."*]

But who is coming?

[**Corin** *enters.*]

Corin [*to* **Celia** *as* **Aliena** *and* **Rosalind** *as* **Ganymede**] Mistress and master, you have often asked me about that shepherd who moaned about being in love, the one you saw sitting beside me on the grass praising the proud, scornful shepherdess who was his sweetheart.

Celia Well, what about him?

Corin If you want to see a real drama played out by a true lover with his pale complexion and a scornful and proud woman with her fiery red cheeks, come with me a little way; I will take you there, if you want to see it.

Rosalind [*to* **Celia**] Oh, yes, let's go! The sight of other lovers is like food to those in love.

[*to* **Corin**] Take us to see this sight, and I'll give you good reason to say that I have been an active participant in their play.

[*They all exit.*]

Scene 5

Enter **Silvius** *and* **Phebe**.

Silvius   Sweet Phebe, do not scorn me, do not,
    Phebe;
  Say that you love me not, but say not so
  In bitterness. The common executioner,
  Whose heart th' accustom'd sight of death makes hard,
5 Falls not the axe upon the humbled neck
  But first begs pardon. Will you sterner be
  Than he that dies and lives by bloody drops?

Enter, [behind,] **Rosalind**, **Celia**, *and* **Corin**.

Phebe   I would not be thy executioner;
  I fly thee for I would not injure thee.
10 Thou tell'st me there is murder in mine eye:
  'Tis pretty, sure, and very probable,
  That eyes, that are the frail'st and softest things,
  Who shut their coward gates on atomies,
  Should be called tyrants, butchers, murtherers!
15 Now I do frown on thee with all my heart,
  And if mine eyes can wound, now let them kill thee.
  Now counterfeit to swound; why, now fall down,
  Or if thou canst not, O, for shame, for shame,
  Lie not, to say mine eyes are murtherers!
20 Now show the wound mine eye hath made in thee;
  Scratch thee but with a pin, and there remains
  Some scar of it; lean upon a rush,
  The cicatrice and capable impressure
  Thy palm some moment keeps; but now mine eyes,
25 Which I have darted at thee, hurt thee not,
  Nor I am sure there is no force in eyes
  That can do hurt.

Scene 5

Another part of the Forest of Arden.

[**Silvius** *and* **Phebe** *enter.*]

Silvius [*weeping and pleading*] Sweet Phebe, don't reject
me! Don't, Phebe! Say that you don't love me, but don't say
it harshly. Even the ordinary executioner, who sees death
so often that his heart is hardened, doesn't just drop the ax
blade upon the neck of the poor criminal without first
asking his forgiveness for doing so. Will you be even more
hardhearted than the one who spends his whole life
earning his living by shedding others' blood?

[**Rosalind** *as* **Ganymede**, **Celia** *as* **Aliena**, *and* **Corin** *enter,
unobserved.*]

Phebe   [*coldly and sarcastically*] I don't want to be your executioner. I avoid you because I don't want to hurt you. You
say that my eye has the power to kill you; that's very clever,
of course, and so believable that eyes, which are the
weakest and softest things, which close their cowardly lids
at the smallest specks of dust, should be called tyrants,
slayers, murderers! Now I'll frown at you as hard as I can; if
my eyes can actually cause injury, let them kill you right
now. Pretend to faint now. Go on, fall down! But, if you
can't do so, shame on you! Don't lie and say that my eyes
are murderers. Go on, show me the wound that my eyes
have made on your body. If someone merely scratches you
with a pin, you'll have a scar from it. Lean on a rush, and
your palm will retain the mark and impression for several
minutes. But my eyes, with which I have stared at you,
haven't injured you. And I'm sure there is no power in
anyone's eyes to hurt someone.

Silvius   O dear Phebe,
If ever (as that ever may be near)
You meet in some fresh cheek the power of fancy,
30   Then shall you know the wounds invisible
That love's keen arrows make.

Phebe   But till that time
Come not thou near me; and when that time comes,
Afflict me with thy mocks, pity me not,
As till that time I shall not pity thee.

Rosalind   [*Advancing.*] And why, I pray you? Who
35   might be your mother,
That you insult, exult, and all at once,
Over the wretched? What though you have no
        beauty—
As, by my faith, I see no more in you
Than without candle may go dark to bed—
40   Must you be therefore proud and pitiless?
Why, what means this? why do you look on me?
I see no more in you than in the ordinary
Of nature's sale-work. 'Od's my little life,
I think she means to tangle my eyes too!
45   No, faith, proud mistress, hope not after it.
'Tis not your inky brows, your black silk hair,
Your bugle eyeballs, nor your cheek of cream
That can entame my spirits to your worship.
You foolish shepherd, wherefore do you follow her,
50   Like foggy south, puffing with wind and rain?
You are a thousand times a properer man
Than she a woman. 'Tis such fools as you
That makes the world full of ill-favor'd children.
'Tis not her glass, but you that flatters her,
55   And out of you she sees herself more proper
Than any of her lineaments can show her.

Silvius [*moaning*] Oh, dear Phebe, if ever in the future—and that future time may be soon—you meet someone young and handsome, and his face has the power to attract you, then you will experience the invisible wounds that the sharp arrows of love make.

Phebe But until that happens, stay away from me, and when it does happen, go on and mock me. Don't feel sorry for me any more than I will feel sorry for you until then.

Rosalind [*striding forward, speaking scornfully as* **Ganymede**] And why, tell me please? Who do you think you are, that you insult and gloat, both at the same time, over this wretched man? You aren't beautiful—really, your beauty isn't even enough to light your way to bed—yet you think you can be proud and pitiless? [*suddenly noticing* **Phebe's** *love-struck expression*] Why, what's this? Why are you looking at me like that? I don't see anything in you that's beyond nature's run-of-the-mill workmanship. God help me, I think she's trying to captivate me, too! [*Seeing that her criticism has not diminished* **Phebe's** *infatuation,* **Rosalind** *tries to discourage her.*] No indeed, proud lady, don't hope for it. Neither your black eyebrows, your silky black hair, your eyes like black beads, nor your creamy cheeks can enslave me and make me worship you.

[*in exasperation, to* **Silvius**] You foolish shepherd, why do you follow her around, sighing like a foggy south wind puffing out gusty sighs and tears like rain? You are a thousand times a better-looking man than she is a woman. It's fools like you that fill the world with ugly children. It's not her mirror that flatters her; it's you! With you as her mirror, she sees herself as being far more attractive than she really is.

But, mistress, know yourself, down on your knees,
And thank heaven, fasting, for a good man's love;
For I must tell you friendly in your ear,
60   Sell when you can, you are not for all markets.
Cry the man mercy, love him, take his offer;
Foul is most foul, being foul to be a scoffer.
So take her to thee, shepherd. Fare you well.

Phebe   Sweet youth, I pray you chide a year together,
65   I had rather hear you chide than this man woo.

Rosalind   He's fall'n in love with your foulness—and
she'll fall in love with my anger. If it be so, as
fast as she answers thee with frowning looks, I'll
sauce her with bitter words.—Why look you so
70   upon me?

Phebe   For no ill will I bear you.

Rosalind   I pray you do not fall in love with me,
For I am falser than vows made in wine.
Besides, I like you not. If you will know my house,
75   'Tis at the tuft of olives here hard by.
Will you go, sister? Shepherd, ply her hard.
Come, sister. Shepherdess, look on him better,
And be not proud; though all the world could see,
None could be so abus'd in sight as he.
80   Come, to our flock.

Exit [*wth* **Celia** *and* **Corin**].

[*sternly, to* **Phebe**] Lady, know yourself. Get down on your knees and thank heaven, fasting, for the love of a good man. For I must give you a friendly warning: You should sell while you have a buyer; you won't be in such demand everywhere. Ask the man's forgiveness. Love him. Accept his proposal. [**Rosalind** *recites a proverb.*] "Ugliness is worst when it is ugly by being scornful."

[*to* **Silvius**] So take her as your wife, shepherd, and good luck.

Phebe [*coyly*] Sweet youth, scold me without stopping for a whole year. I would rather listen to you scold me than hear this man woo me.

Rosalind [*to* **Phebe**] Silvius has fallen in love with your scornfulness.

[*to* **Silvius**] And she's falling in love with my anger. If that's so, just as soon as she answers you with frowns, I'll rebuke her sharply with bitter words.

[*in exasperation, to* **Phebe**] Why are you looking at me like that?

Phebe [*smiling flirtatiously*] Because I don't have any hard feelings toward you.

Rosalind   Please, don't fall in love with me. I'm as false as vows people make when they're drunk. Besides, I don't like you.

[*to* **Silvius**] If you want to find my house, it's near the cluster of olive trees nearby.

[*to* **Celia** *as* **Aliena**] Are you ready to go, sister?

[*to* **Silvius**] Shepherd, try hard to win her.

[*to* **Celia**] Come on, sister.

[*sternly, to* **Phebe**] Shepherdess, look more kindly on him and don't be proud. Even though the whole world has eyes, no one else will be as deceived by his eyes as he is.

[*to* **Celia** *and* **Corin**] Come, let's go check on our sheep.

[**Rosalind, Celia,** *and* **Corin** *leave together.*]

Phebe   Dead shepherd, now I find thy saw of might,
  "Who ever lov'd that lov'd not at first sight?"

Silvius   Sweet Phebe—

Phebe   Hah! what say'st thou, Silvius?

Silvius   Sweet Phebe, pity me.

85 **Phebe**   Why, I am sorry for thee, gentle Silvius.

Silvius   Where ever sorrow is, relief would be.
  If you do sorrow at my grief in love,
  By giving love, your sorrow and my grief
  Were both extermin'd.

Phebe   Thou hast my love; is not that neigh-
90   borly?

Silvius   I would have you.

Phebe   [*sighing gustily*] Dead Shepherd, I understand the power of your saying: "Who ever really loved who didn't fall in love at first sight?" [*Referring to Christopher Marlowe, who died in 1593,* **Phebe** *quotes line 82 from his* Hero and Leander.]

Silvius   Sweet Phebe—

Phebe   [*in irritation at having her thoughts interrupted*] What? What did you say, Silvius?

Silvius   Sweet Phebe, have pity on me.

Phebe   Why, I do feel sorry for you, dear Silvius.

Silvius   [*hopefully*] People who feel sorry for others should want to relieve their suffering. If you feel sorry about my distress in loving you, by loving me in return you could eliminate both your own regret and my distress.

Phebe   You have my friendship. Isn't that being neighborly enough? [**Phebe** *refers to Matthew 19:19, which says,* "Love thy neighbor as thyself."]

Silvius   I want you.

Phebe   Why, that were covetousness.
Silvius, the time was that I hated thee;
And yet it is not that I bear thee love,
But since that thou canst talk of love so well,
95   Thy company, which erst was irksome to me,
I will endure; and I'll employ thee too.
But do not look for further recompense
Than thine own gladness that thou art employ'd.

Silvius   So holy and so perfect is my love,
100   And I in such a poverty of grace,
That I shall think it a most plenteous crop
To glean the broken ears after the man
That the main harvest reaps. Loose now and then
A scatt'red smile, and that I'll live upon.

Phebe   Know'st thou the youth that spoke to me
105   yerwhile?

Silvius   Not very well, but I have met him oft,
And he hath bought the cottage and the bounds
That the old carlot once was master of.

Phebe   Why, that's being covetous. Silvius, at one time I hated you. But because you speak of love so well, even though I don't love you, I will put up with your company, which once was annoying to me. And I'll give you a job to do, too. But don't look for any reward beyond your own happiness that I'm giving you something to do for me. [**Phebe's** *statement about not being "covetous" refers to Exodus 20:17, which says, "Thou shalt not covet thy neighbor's house, thou shalt not covet thy neighbor's wife . . . nor any thing that is thy neighbor's."*]

Silvius   [*with fawning humility*] My love for you is so holy and perfect and I have so little in the way of good fortune that I will think of it as an abundant crop to pick up the fallen ears of corn left by the man who reaps the first harvest. Give me only an occasional smile, and I'll live on that. [*In Leviticus 19:10, the owners of the harvest are told to leave behind some of the crop so that the poor can gather the remnants.*]

Phebe   [*feigning indifference to* **Silvius'** *answer*] Do you know that lad who spoke to me a little while ago?

Silvius   Not very well, but I have seen him often. He has bought the cottage and the lands that the old peasant used to own.

Phebe   Think not I love him, though I ask for him;
110   'Tis but a peevish boy—yet he talks well—
But what care I for words? Yet words do well
When he that speaks them pleases those that hear.
It is a pretty youth—not very pretty—
But sure he's proud—and yet his pride becomes him.
115   He'll make a proper man. The best thing in him
Is his complexion; and faster than his tongue
Did make offense, his eye did heal it up.
He is not very tall—yet for his years he's tall;
His leg is but so so—and yet 'tis well;
120   There was a pretty redness in his lip,
A little riper and more lusty red
Than that mix'd in his cheek; 'twas just the difference
Betwixt the constant red and mingled damask.
There be some women, Silvius, had they mark'd him
125   In parcels as I did, would have gone near
To fall in love with him; but for my part
I love him not, nor hate him not; and yet
Have more cause to hate him than to love him,
For what had he to do to chide at me?
He said mine eyes were black and my hair black,
131   And, now I am rememb'red, scorn'd at me.
I marvel why I answer'd not again.
But that's all one; omittance is no quittance.
I'll write to him a very taunting letter,
135   And thou shalt bear it; wilt thou, Silvius?

Silvius   Phebe, with all my heart.

Phebe   I'll write it straight;
The matter's in my head and in my heart.
I will be bitter with him and passing short.
Go with me, Silvius.

Exeunt.

Phebe Don't think that I love him just because I'm asking about him. He's just a silly boy. But he speaks well. But what do I care about his words? And yet words are good when they are spoken by someone who is pleasing to listen to. He's a good-looking youth. Well, not extremely good-looking. But he certainly is proud. And yet his pride is a good thing in him. He'll be a handsome man. The best thing about him is his appearance. And even faster than his tongue could say something offensive, his handsome eyes made it all right. He's not very tall . . . yet for his age he *is* tall. His legs are only so-so, and yet they are good. His lips were a fine red, a little riper and more luxurious than the red that was in his cheeks; it was the difference between the constant red of his lips and the mixture of red and white in his cheeks. There are some women, Silvius, who, if they had noted his individual features as I did, they would nearly have fallen in love with him. But I neither love nor hate him, for what business did he have scolding me? He said my eyes are black and my hair is black, and now that I think of it, he mocked me. I'm amazed that I didn't tell him off. But it doesn't matter. I might still do so. I'll write him a very insulting letter, and you shall take it to him. Will you, Silvius? [*See bracketed note concerning "black" after Act 3 Scene 2 Line 95.*]

Silvius [*fervently glad to be allowed to serve his beloved* **Phebe**] With all my heart, Phebe.

Phebe I'll write it right away. What I want to say is in my head and my heart. I'll be nasty to him and extremely curt. Come with me, Silvius.

[*They leave.*]

Act four

Scene 1

Enter **Rosalind** *and* **Celia** *and* **Jaques**.

Jaques   I prithee, pretty youth, let me [be] better acquainted with thee.

Rosalind   They say you are a melancholy fellow.

4 **Jaques**   I am so; I do love it better than laughing.

Rosalind   Those that are in extremity of either are abominable fellows, and betray themselves to every modern censure worse than drunkards.

Jaques   Why, 'tis good to be sad and say nothing.

9 **Rosalind**   Why, then, 'tis good to be a post.

Jaques   I have neither the scholar's melancholy, which is emulation; nor the musician's, which is fantastical; nor the courtier's, which is proud; nor the soldier's, which is ambitious; nor the lawyer's, which is politic; nor the lady's, which is nice; nor
15   the lover's, which is all these: but it is a melancholy of mine own, compounded of many simples, extracted from many objects, and indeed the sundry contemplation of my travels, in which [my] often rumination wraps me in a most humorous
20   sadness.

Act four

Scene 1

The Forest of Arden.

[**Jaques, Rosalind** *as* **Ganymede,** *and* **Celia** *as* **Aliena** *enter.*]

Jaques   Please, pretty youth, let me get to know you better.

Rosalind   [*speaking as* **Ganymede**] People say you're a melancholy fellow.

Jaques   I am. I like being melancholy better than laughing.

Rosalind   People who are either extremely gloomy or jolly are detestable, and they expose themselves to common criticism even more than drunkards do.

Jaques   [*defensively*] Why, it's good to be sad and not say anything!

Rosalind   Why then, you might as well be a post.

Jaques   I don't have the type of melancholy that a scholar has who is envious of the accomplishments of others. Nor is it like the musician's, which is temperamental; nor the courtier's, which is proud; nor the soldier's, which is ambitious. It's not like the lawyer's, which is faked; nor the lady's, which is picky; nor the lover's, which is all of these things. It's a melancholy all my own, brewed from many ingredients, extracted from the many things I've seen and from my various experiences while traveling; my frequent contemplation of these things wraps me in a very moody sort of sadness.

Rosalind   A traveller! By my faith, you have great
reason to be sad. I fear you have sold your own
lands to see other men's; then to have seen much,
and to have nothing, is to have rich eyes and poor
25   hands.

Jaques   Yes, I have gain'd my experience.

Enter ORLANDO.

Rosalind   And your experience makes you sad. I had
rather have a fool to make me merry than experience
to make me sad—and to travel for it too!

30 **Orlando**   Good day and happiness, dear Rosalind!

Jaques   Nay, then, God buy you, and you talk in
blank verse.

Rosalind   Farewell, Monsieur Traveller: look you
lisp and wear strange suits; disable all the benefits of
35   your own country; be out of love with your
nativity, and almost chide God for making you
that countenance you are; or I will scarce think
you have swam in a gundello. [*Exit* **Jaques**.] Why,
how now, Orlando, where have you been all this
while? You a lover! An you serve me such another
41   trick, never come in my sight more.

Rosalind   You're a traveler! Then you certainly do have great reason to be sad. I'm afraid that you've sold your own lands to go see those belonging to other men. If you have seen a lot and own nothing, then you have eyes that are rich but hands that are poor.

Jaques   Yes, but I have gained my experience.

Rosalind   And yet your experience makes you sad. I would rather have a jester to cheer me up than experience to make me sad—and you had to travel to get it, too!

[**Orlando** *enters.*]

Orlando   [*speaking to* **Rosalind** *who is masquerading as* **Ganymede** *pretending to be* **Rosalind**] Good day and may you be happy, dear Rosalind.

[**Rosalind** *hears his greeting but pretends not to.*]

Jaques   [*to* **Orlando**] No, then, I'm leaving if you're going to talk in blank verse. [*Blank verse is unrhymed iambic pentameter. An iamb is a poetic unit, called a "foot," consisting of an unstressed beat followed by a stressed beat. Pentameter is a line of poetry consisting of five poetic feet.*]

[**Jaques** *leaves.*]

Rosalind   [*to* **Jaques**] Goodbye, Monsieur Traveler. Be sure to pretend you have a foreign accent, wear outlandish outfits, criticize all the benefits of your own country, dislike your own nationality, and practically scold God for making you look like an Englishman, or I will find it hard to believe that you have ever floated in a gondola. [**Rosalind** *is mocking the typical conduct of English travelers once they return home.*]

[*still as* **Ganymede**, *pretending to notice* **Orlando** *for the first time*] Why, hello, Orlando! Where have you been all this time? You claim to be a lover? If you treat me like this again, don't ever come see me anymore.

Orlando   My fair Rosalind, I come within an hour of
my promise.

Rosalind   Break an hour's promise in love! He that
45 will divide a minute into a thousand parts, and
break but a part of the thousand part of a minute
in the affairs of love, it may be said of him that
Cupid hath clapp'd him o' th' shoulder, but I'll
warrant him heart-whole.

50 **Orlando**   Pardon me, dear Rosalind.

Rosalind   Nay, and you be so tardy, come no more in
my sight. I had as lief be woo'd of a snail.

Orlando   Of a snail?

Rosalind   Ay, of a snail; for though he comes slowly,
55 he carries his house on his head; a better jointure I think than you make a woman. Besides,
he brings his destiny with him.

Orlando   What's that?

Rosalind   Why, horns! which such as you are fain to
60 be beholding to your wives for. But he comes
arm'd in his fortune, and prevents the slander of
his wife.

Orlando   Virtue is no horn-maker; and my Rosalind
is virtuous.

65 **Rosalind**   And I am your Rosalind.

Celia   It pleases him to call you so; but he hath a
Rosalind of a better leer than you.

Orlando   [*sheepishly*] My beautiful Rosalind, I'm here within an hour of when I said I would be.

Rosalind   You would break your promise as a lover by a whole hour! If someone would divide a minute into a thousand parts and then break so much as a thousandth of one minute in things concerning his love, you could say that Cupid's arrow has grazed his shoulder, but I'll guarantee that his heart hasn't been touched.

Orlando   Forgive me, Rosalind.

Rosalind   No, if you're going to be so late, don't come see me again. I would rather be wooed by a snail.

Orlando   By a snail?

Rosalind   Yes, by a snail, because even though he is slow, he carries his house on his head, which is a better jointure, I think, than what you would give to a woman. Besides, he brings his destiny with him. [*A jointure is the property a woman received as a marriage settlement in case of her husband's death.*]

Orlando   What fate is that?

Rosalind   Why, horns, which men such as you are forced to receive from your wives. But he comes already wearing his horns and thereby prevents the disgrace his wife would bring him. [**Rosalind** *refers to the cuckold's horns. Since the snail already has horns (antennae, that is), no one would notice if he wore the horns of the cuckold.*]

Orlando   Virtuous women don't cause their husbands to wear horns, and my Rosalind is virtuous.

Rosalind   And I am your Rosalind.

Celia   [*interrupting, as* **Aliena**] He has chosen to call you that, but he has a better-looking Rosalind than you.

Rosalind   Come, woo me, woo me; for now I am in a
holiday humor, and like enough to consent. What
would you say to me now, and I were your very very
71   Rosalind?

Orlando   I would kiss before I spoke.

Rosalind   Nay, you were better speak first, and when
you were gravell'd for lack of matter, you might
75   take occasion to kiss. Very good orators when
they are out, they will spit, and for lovers lacking
(God warn us!) matter, the cleanliest shift is to kiss.

Orlando   How if the kiss be denied?

Rosalind   Then she puts you to entreaty, and there
80   begins new matter.

Orlando   Who could be out, being before his belov'd
mistress?

Rosalind   Marry, that should you if I were your mistress, or I should think my honesty ranker than
85   my wit.

Orlando   What, of my suit?

Rosalind   Not out of your apparel, and yet out of your
suit. Am not I your Rosalind?

Orlando   I take some joy to say you are, because I
90   would be talking of her.

Rosalind [*to* **Orlando**, *ignoring the interruption*] Come, woo me! Woo me! I'm in a good mood and likely to accept your proposal. What would you say to me now if I really and truly were your Rosalind?

Orlando I would kiss you before I said anything.

Rosalind [*considering his suggestion*] No, you had better talk first and when you run out of things to talk about, then you could take the opportunity to kiss. Very good orators, when they run out of things to say, will spit. And when lovers run out—God help us!—of conversation, the smartest thing to do is kiss. [**Rosalind**, *in using the word "cleanliest," is making a play on words also referring to the cleanliness of kissing versus spitting.*]

Orlando What if she refuses to kiss me?

Rosalind Then she forces you to beg, which gives you something new to talk about.

Orlando Who could run out of things to say while looking at the woman he loves?

Rosalind You would, actually, if I were your sweetheart, or I would think my chastity stinks compared to my cleverness. [**Rosalind's** *joke makes reference to her earlier discussion with* **Celia** *about Fortune usually making women who are sexually pure ugly. (See Act 1 Scene 2 Lines 37–39.)*]

Orlando What, out of my suit? [*"Suit" refers to his courtship of* **Rosalind**.]

Rosalind [*using two meanings for "suit"*] You wouldn't be without your suit, yet you would have to give up your suit. Am I your Rosalind?

Orlando It gives me a certain amount of happiness to say that you are because I like to talk about her.

Rosalind   Well in her person, I say I will not have you.

Orlando   Then in mine own person, I die.

Rosalind   No, faith, die by attorney. The poor world
is almost six thousand years old, and in all this
96   time there was not any man died in his own
person, *videlicet*, in a love-cause. Troilus had his
brains dash'd out with a Grecian club, yet he did
what he could to die before, and he is one of the
100   patterns of love. Leander, he would have liv'd
many a fair year though Hero had turn'd nun, if it
had not been for a hot midsummer night; for, good
youth, he went but forth to wash him in the Hellespont,
and being taken with the cramp was drown'd; and
105   the foolish chroniclers of that age found it was—
Hero of Sestos. But these are all lies: men have died
from time to time, and worms have eaten them,
but not for love.

Orlando   I would not have my right Rosalind of this
110   mind, for I protest her frown might kill me.

Rosalind   By this hand, it will not kill a fly. But
come, now I will be your Rosalind in a more com-
ing-on disposition; and ask me what you will, I will
grant it.

115 **Orlando**   Then love me, Rosalind.

Rosalind   Yes, faith, will I, Fridays and Saturdays and
all.

Rosalind   Well, speaking for her, I won't have you.

Orlando   Then, speaking for myself, I will die.

Rosalind   No, don't do that; let a lawyer stand in for you when you die. This poor world is almost six thousand years old, yet in all this time not a single man actually died for the sake of love. Troilus had his head smashed in by the club of a Greek, yet he had tried his best to die for love before that, and he is considered an exemplary lover. Leander would have lived many happy years, even if Hero had become a nun, if it hadn't been for one hot midsummer night. He went, fine youth that he was, to take a bath in the Hellespont and developed a cramp and drowned, yet the foolish coroners gave the cause of his death as "Hero of Sestos." But these stories are all lies. Men have died from time to time, and worms have eaten them, but they haven't died because of love. [*The age of the earth, based on the generations listed in the Bible, was believed to be about 6000 years at that time. Troilus died in battle after his lover, Cressida, was unfaithful to him; Leander drowned when a tempest arose as he was trying to swim the Hellespont to be with Hero, a priestess to Venus. However,* **Rosalind** *presents the deaths of the legendary lovers as unromantically as possible.*]

Orlando   I wouldn't want my actual Rosalind to think as you do, for, I swear to you, she could kill me by frowning at me.

Rosalind   [*raising her hand as if taking an oath*] And I swear to you that her frown wouldn't even kill a fly. But, come, I'll be your Rosalind in a more encouraging mood. Ask me whatever you like, and I will grant it.

Orlando   Then love me, Rosalind.

Rosalind   Yes, indeed, I will, on Fridays and Saturdays and every day.

Orlando   And wilt thou have me?

Rosalind   Ay, and twenty such.

120 **Orlando**   What sayest thou?

Rosalind   Are you not good?

Orlando   I hope so.

Rosalind   Why then, can one desire too much of a
good thing? Come, sister, you shall be the priest,
and marry us. Give me your hand, Orlando. What
126   do you say, sister?

Orlando   Pray thee, marry us.

Celia   I cannot say the words.

Rosalind   You must begin, "Will you, Orlando"—

Celia   Go to! Will you, Orlando, have to wife this
131   Rosalind?

Orlando   I will.

Rosalind   Ay, but when?

Orlando   Why, now, as fast as she can marry us.

Rosalind   Then you must say, "I take thee, Rosalind,
136   for wife."

Orlando   I take thee, Rosalind, for wife.

Orlando   And will you have me?

Rosalind   Yes, and twenty others like you. [*She implies that she will be unfaithful to him even though she has no such intention.*]

Orlando   [*shocked*] What do you mean?

Rosalind   Aren't you good?

Orlando   I hope so.

Rosalind   Why, then, is it possible to want too much of something good?

[*to* **Celia** *as* **Aliena**] Come, sister, you pretend to be the priest and marry us.

[*to* **Orlando**] Give me your hand, Orlando.

[*to* **Celia** *as* **Aliena**] Will you do it, sister?

Orlando   [*to* "**Aliena**"] Please, marry us.

Celia   I can't say the words. [*She seems to be reminding* **Rosalind** *that, because she isn't a priest, the marriage will not be binding.*]

Rosalind   You must begin, "Will you, Orlando—"

Celia   [*impatiently*] Okay, okay! Will you, Orlando, take this Rosalind as your wife?

Orlando   I will.

Rosalind   Yes, but when?

Orlando   Why, now, as fast as she can marry us.

Rosalind   Then you must say, "I take you, Rosalind, as my wife."

Orlando   [*obediently repeating her words*] I take you, Rosalind, as my wife.

Rosalind   I might ask you for your commission, but
I do take thee, Orlando, for my husband. There's
a girl goes before the priest, and certainly a woman's
141   thought runs before her actions.

Orlando   So do all thoughts, they are wing'd.

Rosalind   Now tell me how long you would have her
after you have possess'd her.

145 **Orlando**   For ever and a day.

Rosalind   Say "a day," without the "ever." No, no,
Orlando, men are April when they woo, December
when they wed; maids are May when they are maids,
but the sky changes when they are wives. I will
150   be more jealous of thee than a Barbary cock-
pigeon over his hen, more clamorous than a parrot
against rain, more new-fangled than an ape, more
giddy in my desires than a monkey. I will weep for
nothing, like Diana in the fountain, and I will do that
155   when you are dispos'd to be merry. I will laugh
like a hyen, and that when thou art inclin'd to sleep.

Orlando   But will my Rosalind do so?

Rosalind   By my life, she will do as I do.

159 **Orlando**   O, but she is wise.

Rosalind   I should ask you for the license — but I do take you, Orlando, for my husband. The girl got ahead of the priest, but then a woman's thoughts run faster than her actions. [*Realizing that the "priest" hasn't yet asked her to repeat the bride's vow,* **Rosalind** *mocks her own eagerness to respond.*]

Orlando   All thoughts do; they have wings.

Rosalind   Now tell me how long you would keep her after you have had her. [*"Had" refers to marriage as well to having intercourse.*]

Orlando   [*fervently*] Forever and a day.

Rosalind   Just say "a day," without the "forever." No, no, Orlando, men are as full of promise as April when they are wooing but as cold as December when they are married; when girls are single, they're like a delightful day in May, but the weather changes when they are wives. I'll be more jealous of you than a male Barbary pigeon over his hen, more noisy than a parrot just before it rains, more obsessed with new things than an ape, and more changeable about my demands than a monkey. I'll cry for no reason, like a statue of Diana in a fountain, and I'll do it when you feel like having fun. And I'll laugh like a hyena when you're trying to go to sleep. [*Barbary cock-pigeons were known for being possessive of their mates.* **Rosalind's** *reference to the statue of Diana may refer to the shepherd in Montemayor's* Diana, *in which Diana, the faithless beloved of the shepherd, wept into a fountain while she falsely vowed to be true to him forever.*]

Orlando   But will *my* Rosalind do that?

Rosalind   I swear to you that she'll act just as I do.

Orlando   But she is wise.

Rosalind   Or else she could not have the wit to do
this; the wiser, the waywarder. Make the doors
upon a woman's wit, and it will out at the casement;
shut that, and 'twill out at the key-hole; stop that,
'twill fly with the smoke out at the chimney.

Orlando   A man that had a wife with such a wit, he
166   might say, "Wit, whither wilt?"

Rosalind   Nay, you might keep that check for it, till
you met your wive's wit going to your neighbor's
bed.

Orlando   And what wit could wit have to excuse that?

Rosalind   Marry, to say she came to seek you there.
172   You shall never take her without her answer,
unless you take her without her tongue. O, that
woman that cannot make her fault her husband's
occasion, let her never nurse her child herself, for
176   she will breed it like a fool!

Orlando   For these two hours, Rosalind, I will leave
thee.

Rosalind   Alas, dear love, I cannot lack thee two hours!

Orlando   I must attend the Duke at dinner. By two
a' clock I will be with thee again.

Rosalind   Ay, go your ways, go your ways; I knew
183   what you would prove; my friends told me as
much, and I thought no less. That flattering tongue
of yours won me. 'Tis but one cast away, and so
come death! Two a' clock is your hour?

Rosalind   If she weren't, she wouldn't be smart enough to act like this. The wiser a woman is, the more difficult she is. Lock the doors on a woman's wit, and it will dart out the window; shut that and it will slip out the keyhole; plug that up and it will fly up the chimney with the smoke.

Orlando   If a man had a wife like that, he might say, "Wit, where do you wander?" [*a proverbial saying meaning, "Fool, what can you be thinking?"*]

Rosalind   No, you had better keep that rebuke for when you catch your wife in your neighbor's bed.

Orlando   And what ingenious excuse could even a clever woman have for that?

Rosalind   Why, to say that she was looking for *you* there. You will never catch her without an answer unless you catch her without her tongue. Don't let the woman who can't blame her own fault on something her husband has done breast-feed her own baby, for she'll turn it into a fool! [**Rosalind** *refers to the belief that a child would receive either wisdom or foolishness in the milk of its mother.*]

Orlando   I need to leave you for two hours, Rosalind.

Rosalind   [*speaking melodramatically to hide her genuine disappointment*] Alas, dear love, I can't bear to be separated from you for two hours!

Orlando   I have to go have dinner with the duke. I'll be with you again by two o'clock.

Rosalind   Oh, yes, go on! Leave! I knew what you would turn out to be. My friends warned me, and I thought so, too. But your flattery won me over. I'm just one more rejected woman, so I might as well be dead! You'll be back at two o'clock?

187 **Orlando**   Ay, sweet Rosalind.

Rosalind   By my troth, and in good earnest, and so
God mend me, and by all pretty oaths that are not
dangerous, if you break one jot of your promise, or
come one minute behind your hour, I will think
you the most pathetical break-promise, and the
193 most hollow lover, and the most unworthy of her
you call Rosalind, that may be chosen out of the
gross band of the unfaithful; therefore beware my
censure, and keep your promise.

Orlando   With no less religion than if thou wert indeed
198 my Rosalind; so adieu.

Rosalind   Well, Time is the old justice that examines
all such offenders, and let Time try. Adieu.

Exit [**Orlando**].

Celia   You have simply misus'd our sex in your love-
202 prate. We must have your doublet and hose
pluck'd over your head, and show the world what
the bird hath done to her own nest.

Rosalind   O coz, coz, coz, my pretty little coz, that
206 thou didst know how many fathom deep I am
in love! But it cannot be sounded; my affection
hath an unknown bottom, like the bay of Portugal.

Celia   Or rather, bottomless—that as fast as you
pour affection in, [it] runs out.

Orlando Yes, sweet Rosalind.

Rosalind I swear, and I mean this, so help me God, by all fine vows that are not blasphemous, if you break your oath by as much as an iota or come one minute late, I will think you are the most miserable promise-breaker and the most insincere lover and the person most unworthy of the woman you call "Rosalind" that could be found among the whole group of unfaithful lovers. So beware of my disapproval and keep your promise.

Orlando I will, with no less faithfulness than if you really were my Rosalind. So, goodbye.

Rosalind Well, Time is the old judge who puts those who are late on trial, so we'll leave it to him to decide your case. Goodbye.

[**Orlando** *leaves.*]

Celia [*indignantly*] You've completely slandered our gender in your love-rant! We ought to have your clothing pulled off to show the world that it's a woman who is being so disloyal to other women. [**Celia** *refers to an old proverb that says, "It is a foul bird that defiles its own nest."*]

Rosalind [*groaning*] Oh, coz, coz, coz, my pretty little coz, if you only knew how many fathoms deep I am in love! But it's too deep to measure; the bottom of my love, like the Bay of Portugal, is so deep that it can't be found. [*A fathom is a nautical unit of measurement equal to six feet.*]

Celia [*dryly*] Or maybe the bottom doesn't exist, so that as quickly as you pour your love into it, it all runs out again.

Rosalind   No, that same wicked bastard of Venus
212   that was begot of thought, conceiv'd of spleen, and
born of madness, that blind rascally boy that abuses
every one's eyes because his own are out, let him be
judge how deep I am in love. I'll tell thee, Aliena,
I cannot be out of the sight of Orlando. I'll go find
217   a shadow, and sigh till he come.

Celia   And I'll sleep.

Exeunt.

Scene 2

Enter **Jaques** *and* **Lords** [*as*] *foresters.*

Jaques   Which is he that kill'd the deer?

First Lord   Sir, it was I.

Jaques   Let's present him to the Duke like a Roman
conqueror, and it would do well to set the deer's horns
upon his head, for a branch of victory. Have you
6   no song, forester, for this purpose?

Second Lord   Yes, sir.

Jaques   Sing it. 'Tis no matter how it be in tune,
so it make noise enough.

Music.

Rosalind   No, let Cupid—the same wicked bastard child of
Venus, who was conceived as a result of infatuation and
impulse, and born because of extreme folly, that blind mis-
chievous boy who plays tricks on everyone else's eyes
because he can't see—be the judge of how deeply I am in
love. I assure you, Celia, that I can't stand to be apart from
Orlando. I'll go find a shady place and sigh until he returns.

Celia   And I'm going to go take a nap.

[*They leave separately.*]

Scene 2

The Forest of Arden.

[**Jaques** *and* **Lords** *dressed as foresters enter.*]

Jaques   Which one of you killed the deer?

First Lord   It was I, sir.

Jaques   [*enthusiastically, to others*] Let's present this man to
the duke, like a Roman conqueror. We should set the deer's
horns on his head as a sign of victory. [*A Roman conqueror
would be awarded a wreath to wear on his head like a
crown.*]

[*to* **Second Lord**] Don't you know any suitable song, forester,
for this celebration?

Second Lord   Yes, sir.

Jaques   Sing it. It doesn't matter if it's in tune as long as it's
loud enough.

SONG

Second Lord   What shall he have that kill'd the deer?
11   His leather skin and horns to wear.
          Then sing him home,
            The rest shall bear this burthen.
          Take thou no scorn to wear the horn,
          It was a crest ere thou wast born;
15   Thy father's father wore it,
          And thy father bore it.
          The horn, the horn, the lusty horn
          Is not a thing to laugh to scorn.

Exeunt.

Scene 3

Enter **Rosalind** *and* **Celia**.

Rosalind   How say you now? Is it not past two a'
clock? And here much Orlando!

Celia   I warrant you, with pure love and troubled
brain, he hath ta'en his bow and arrows and is gone
5   forth—to sleep. Look who comes here.

Enter **Silvius**.

Second Lord   [*singing*] *What shall the man have who killed the deer?*

> *The deer's skin and horns to wear.*
> *Then sing to send him home.*

[*The rest of the* **Lords** *pick up the carcass.*]

> *Don't be ashamed to wear the horns;*
> *They were a noble sign before you were born.*
> *Your grandfather wore them,*
> *And your father did as well.*
> *The horn, the horn, the lusty horn*
> *Is not something to mock and scorn.*

[*The "crest" to which the song refers is both the crest on the forehead of the deer and also a coat of arms.*]

[*They all leave together in a procession of victory.*]

Scene 3

The Forest of Arden.

[**Rosalind**, *dressed as* **Ganymede**, *and* **Celia**, *dressed as* **Aliena**, *enter.*]

Rosalind   What do you say now? Isn't it after two o'clock? And Orlando's not here.

Celia   [*sarcastically*] I'll bet you that he, with his perfect love and worried mind, has taken his bow and arrows, and gone off to sleep. [**Celia** *means that* **Orlando** *probably is pretending to have gone hunting but, unlike true lovers who often can't sleep because of thinking about their sweethearts, he's actually taking a nap.*]

Look who's coming this way.

[**Silvius** *enters.*]

Silvius   My errand is to you, fair youth,
My gentle Phebe did bid me give you this.

[*Gives a letter.*]

I know not the contents, but as I guess
By the stern brow and waspish action
10   Which she did use as she was writing of it,
It bears an angry tenure. Pardon me,
I am but as a guiltless messenger.

Rosalind   Patience herself would startle at this letter,
And play the swaggerer: bear this, bear all!
15   She says I am not fair, that I lack manners;
She calls me proud, and that she could not love me
Were man as rare as phoenix. 'Od's my will,
Her love is not the hare that I do hunt;
Why writes she so to me? Well, shepherd, well,
20   This is a letter of your own device.

Silvius   No, I protest, I know not the contents,
Phebe did write it.

Silvius   [*to* "**Ganymede**," *handing him a letter*] I've come to find you, handsome youth. My gentle Phebe told me to give this to you. I don't know what it says, but, based on the frown on her face and the furious way she wrote it, I would guess that it contains an angry message. Forgive me. I'm just the innocent messenger.

Rosalind   [*as* **Ganymede**, *impatiently*] Patience herself would be shocked to get this letter and would want to pick a fight. If I can stand this, I can stand anything. [*She reads the letter.*] She says I am not handsome and that I have bad manners. She says I'm conceited and that she could never love me even if men were as hard to find as a phoenix. Oh, my God! I do nothing to try to make her love me! Why is she writing like this to me? [*suddenly thinking of another explanation for the letter*] A very good try, shepherd. You wrote this letter yourself. [*The phoenix is a mythical bird, only one of which existed at any time, that cremated itself and then was reborn from the ashes of the fire that had consumed it.*]

Silvius   No, really, I don't even know what it says! Phebe wrote it.

Rosalind   Come, come, you are a fool,
And turn'd into the extremity of love.
I saw her hand, she has a leathern hand.
25   A freestone-colored hand. I verily did think
That her old gloves were on, but 'twas her hands;
She has a huswive's hand—but that's no matter.
I say she never did invent this letter,
This is a man's invention and his hand.

30 **Silvius**   Sure it is hers.

Rosalind   Why, 'tis a boisterous and a cruel style,
A style for challengers. Why, she defies me,
Like Turk to Christian. Women's gentle brain
Could not drop forth such giant-rude invention,
35   Such Ethiop words, blacker in their effect
Than in their countenance. Will you hear the letter?

Silvius   So please you, for I never heard it yet;
Yet heard too much of Phebe's cruelty.

Rosalind   She Phebes me. Mark how the tyrant writes.
40   (*Read.*)   "Art thou god to shepherd turn'd,
That a maiden's heart hath burn'd?"
Can a woman rail thus?

Silvius   Call you this railing?

Rosalind   Come, come, you're a fool and love has forced you to extreme measures. I saw her hands. She has leathery, brown skin; I thought for a moment that she had her old gloves on, but they were her hands. They were as work-roughened as a housewife's, but it doesn't matter. I tell you that she didn't write this letter; it was made up by a man and it's a man's handwriting.

Silvius   [*insistently*] Really, she wrote it!

Rosalind   [*shaking her head*] No, it's a rough and rude style, like someone trying to pick a fight. Why, she rebukes me like a Turk would a Christian. A woman's gentle mind couldn't have come out with such incredibly rude ideas, even nastier in meaning than in the ugly way they look on the page. Would you like to hear the letter? [*A popular old Christmas play included a Turkish knight who would challenge St. George, a Christian knight, to combat.*]

Silvius   Yes, please, for I haven't heard it yet—although I *have* heard too much of Phebe's cruelty.

Rosalind   She berates me in typical Phebe style. Listen to what the tyrant writes [*She reads aloud.*]

> "Are you a god transformed into a shepherd,
> That you have set my heart on fire?"

[*commenting to* **Silvius**] Could a woman actually rant like this?

Silvius   You call this ranting?

Rosalind   (*Read.*)
        "Why, thy godhead laid apart,
45   Warr'st thou with a woman's heart?"
  Did you ever hear such railing?
        "Whiles the eye of man did woo me,
        That could do no vengeance to me."
  Meaning me a beast.
50   "If the scorn of your bright eyne
        Have power to raise such love in mine,
        Alack, in me what strange effect
        Would they work in mild aspect?
        Whiles you chid me, I did love;
55   How then might your prayers move?
        He that brings this love to thee
        Little knows this love in me;
        And by him seal up thy mind,
        Whether that thy youth and kind
60   Will the faithful offer take
        Of me, and all that I can make,
        Or else by him my love deny,
        And then I'll study how to die."

Silvius   Call you this chiding?

65 **Celia**   Alas, poor shepherd!

Rosalind   [*alternately reading aloud and commenting*]

> "Why, having laid aside your divinity,
> Do you make war on a woman's heart?"

[*commenting again to* **Silvius**] Did you ever hear such ranting?

> "When other men looked flirtatiously at me,
> They had no effect upon me."

She's saying that I'm not a man, so that must mean I'm an animal. [**Rosalind** *deliberately misinterprets* **Phebe's** *words to spare* **Silvius'** *feelings.*]

> "If the scorn from your bright eyes
> Has such power to make me love you,
> Alas, what strong power would they have
> If they held a kind expression!
> While you reproached me, I fell in love with you;
> How much more love might your wooing cause!
> The man who brings this love letter to you
> Doesn't know that I love you.
> Have him bring me a sealed letter telling me what
>   you think.
> Say whether a young man like you
> Will take my sincere offer
> Of myself and all that I can do,
> Or else say in the letter that you reject my love,
> And then I'll have to think of some way to die."

Silvius   [*in dismay*] You call this ranting?

Celia   Oh, poor shepherd!

Rosalind   Do you pity him? No, he deserves no pity.
Wilt thou love such a woman? What, to make thee
an instrument, and play false strains upon thee! not
to be endur'd! Well, go your way to her (for I see
love hath made thee a tame snake) and say this to her:
that if she love me, I charge her to love thee; if she
will not, I will never have her unless thou entreat for
her. If you be a true lover, hence, and not a word;
for here comes more company.

Exit **Silvius**.

Enter **Oliver**.

Oliver   Good morrow, fair ones. Pray you (if you
know)
Where in the purlieus of this forest stands
A sheep-cote fenc'd about with olive-trees?

Celia   West of this place, down in the neighbor
bottom,
The rank of osiers by the murmuring stream
Left on your right hand brings you to the place.
But at this hour the house doth keep itself,
There's none within.

Oliver   If that an eye may profit by a tongue,
Then should I know you by description—
Such garments and such years. "The boy is fair,
Of female favor, and bestows himself
Like a ripe sister; the woman low,
And browner than her brother." Are not you
The owner of the house I did inquire for?

Rosalind   [*to* **Celia**] Do you pity him? No, he doesn't deserve pity.

[*to* **Silvius**, *in exasperation*] Why do you love such a woman? So that she can play bad tunes on you as if you were an instrument? It's disgusting! Well, go on back to her, for I can see that love has turned you into a pet snake. Tell her this: If she loves me, I order her to love you. If she won't, I will never have her unless *you* beg me to. If you're a true lover, go away, and be silent, for someone is coming. [*Calling someone a "tame snake" was an insult comparable to saying someone is a "wimp."*]

[**Silvius** *leaves looking distressed.* **Oliver** *enters from another direction.*]

Oliver   [*courteously*] Good morning, pretty ones. Please tell me, if you know—Where is the shepherd's cottage surrounded by olive trees that stands in the cleared land at the edge of the forest?

Celia   [*staring at* **Oliver** *in love-struck amazement*] West of here, down in the neighboring dell. Pass the row of willows by the murmuring stream on your right side, and you will come to the place. But the house is looking after itself at this hour; there is no one there.

Oliver   [*returning* "**Aliena's**" *gaze*] If one may benefit from what one has heard, I think I recognize you by your description. You're wearing similar clothing and are about the right age: "The boy is good-looking, with rather feminine features, and carries himself like an older sister. The woman is short and has a more brownish complexion than her brother." Aren't you the owners of the house I was asking about?

90 **Celia**   It is no boast, being ask'd, to say we are.

Oliver   Orlando doth commend him to you both,
And to that youth he calls his Rosalind
He sends this bloody napkin. Are you he?

Rosalind   I am. What must we understand by this?

Oliver   Some of my shame, if you will know of me
96   What man I am, and how, and why, and where
This handkercher was stain'd.

Celia   I pray you tell it.

Oliver   When last the young Orlando parted from you
He left a promise to return again
100   Within an hour, and pacing through the forest,
Chewing the food of sweet and bitter fancy,
Lo what befell! He threw his eye aside,
And mark what object did present itself
Under an old oak, whose boughs were moss'd with
       age
105   And high top bald with dry antiquity:
A wretched ragged man, o'ergrown with hair,
Lay sleeping on his back; about his neck
A green and gilded snake had wreath'd itself,
Who with her head nimble in threats approach'd
110   The opening of his mouth; but suddenly
Seeing Orlando, it unlink'd itself,
And with indented glides did slip away
Into a bush, under which bush's shade
A lioness, with udders all drawn dry,
Lay couching, head on ground, with cat-like watch
116   When that the sleeping man should stir; for 'tis
The royal disposition of that beast
.   To prey on nothing that doth seem as dead.
This seen, Orlando did approach the man,
120   And found it was his brother, his elder brother.

Celia   Since you asked, it's not boasting to say that we are.

Oliver   Orlando greets you both, and he sends this bloody handkerchief to the youth that he calls his "Rosalind." [*He shows them a bloody handkerchief.*]

[*to* **Rosalind**] Is that you?

Rosalind   [*faintly*] I am. What is this handkerchief supposed to tell us?

Oliver   [*hesitantly*] In part, it's about my shame. If you wish, I will tell you who I am, and how and why and where this handkerchief became stained.

Celia   Please, tell us about it.

Oliver   When young Orlando left you, he promised to return within an hour. As he was walking through the forest, meditating on both sweet and bitter thoughts of love, here's what happened. He glanced over to the side—now pay attention to what caught his eye—and he saw a wretched man dressed in rags, with long, shaggy hair, sleeping on his back under an oak with branches mossy with age and its very top so ancient that it was dry and bare. A green and gold snake had wrapped itself around his neck; her head was moving, with darting tongue, toward his open mouth. But suddenly, seeing Orlando, it uncoiled itself and slithered away, slipping into a bush. Under the shade of the bush, a hungry lioness, with her mammaries sucked dry, lay crouching with her head on the ground. Since the royal nature of the beast will not allow it to prey on something that seems dead, the lioness was waiting, as cats do, to see if the sleeping man would move. Seeing all this, Orlando approached the man and saw that he was his brother, his elder brother.

Celia   O, I have heard him speak of that same brother,
And he did render him the most unnatural
That liv'd amongst men.

Oliver   And well he might so do,
For well I know he was unnatural.

125 **Rosalind**   But to Orlando: did he leave him there,
Food to the suck'd and hungry lioness?

Oliver   Twice did he turn his back, and purpos'd so;
But kindness, nobler ever than revenge,
And nature, stronger than his just occasion,
130 Made him give battle to the lioness,
Who quickly fell before him, in which hurtling
From miserable slumber I awaked.

Celia   Are you his brother?

Rosalind   Was't you he rescu'd?

Celia   Was't you that did so oft contrive to kill him?

135 **Oliver**   'Twas I; but 'tis not I. I do not shame
To tell you what I was, since my conversion
So sweetly tastes, being the thing I am.

Rosalind   But for the bloody napkin?

Celia   Oh, yes, I've heard him talk about that brother. He said that there's no man alive as completely lacking in natural brotherly affection as he is.

Oliver   He was correct in saying that, as I can confirm.

Rosalind   But what about Orlando? Did he leave his brother there to be food for the dry and hungry lioness?

Oliver   Twice he turned his back and started to walk away, but his family loyalty was stronger than his desire for revenge, and his natural bond as a brother more powerful than his desire to get even. He fought the lioness and quickly defeated her. The fight awoke me from my miserable slumber.

Celia   [*in dismayed realization*] Are you his brother?

Rosalind   Was it you he rescued?

Celia   [*shocked and shaken*] Was it you who tried so many times to kill him?

Oliver   It was, but I'm not the same person I was. My change of heart is so sweet to me that I'm not ashamed to tell you what I was now that I'm so different.

Rosalind   [*anxiously*] But what about the bloody handkerchief?

Oliver   By and by.
When from the first to last betwixt us two
140   Tears our recountments had most kindly bath'd,
As how I came into that desert place—
[In] brief, he led me to the gentle Duke,
Who gave me fresh array and entertainment,
Committing me unto my brother's love,
145   Who led me instantly unto his cave,
There stripp'd himself, and here upon his arm
The lioness had torn some flesh away,
Which all this while had bled; and now he fainted,
And cried in fainting upon Rosalind.
150   Brief, I recover'd him, bound up his wound,
And after some small space, being strong at heart,
He sent me hither, stranger as I am,
To tell this story, that you might excuse
His broken promise, and to give this napkin
155   Dy'd in [his] blood, unto the shepherd youth
That he in sport doth call his Rosalind.

                                    [**Rosalind** *faints.*]

Celia   Why, how now, Ganymed, sweet Ganymed?

Oliver   Many will swoon when they do look on blood.

Celia   There is more in it. Cousin Ganymed!

160 **Oliver**   Look, he recovers.

Rosalind   I would I were at home.

Celia   We'll lead you thither.
I pray you, will you take him by the arm?

Oliver   Be of good cheer, youth. You a man?
You lack a man's heart.

Oliver I'll get to that in a moment. When, with tears, we had told one another all that had happened to each of us and I had explained how I came to be in that uninhabited place, he took me to the gracious duke, who gave me clean clothing and food to eat and then placed me in my brother's care. Orlando immediately led me to his cave, where he took off his clothes, and he had a wound on his arm from the lioness, which had torn away some of his flesh. The wound had been bleeding all that time, so now he fainted, crying out, "Rosalind!" as he did so. To be brief, I revived him and bound up his wound. He's strong both in courage and body, so after a short time he sent me here, although I'm a stranger to you, to tell you what happened so that you might excuse him for breaking his promise and to show this handkerchief stained with his blood to you, the shepherd youth he jokingly calls his "Rosalind."

[**Rosalind** *faints.*]

Celia [*in distress, falling to her knees beside* **Rosalind**] Are you all right, Ganymede? Dear Ganymede!

Oliver Many people faint when they see blood.

Celia There's more to it than that.

[*to* **Rosalind**] Cousin Ganymede! [*In her anxiety,* **Celia** *forgets to call* **Rosalind** *"brother."*]

Oliver Look, he's recovering.

Rosalind [*woozily*] I wish I were home.

Celia We'll take you there.

[*to* **Oliver**] Please, will you take him by the arm?

Oliver Take heart, lad. You call yourself a man? You don't have a man's courage.

Rosalind   I do so, I confess it. Ah, sirrah, a body
166   would think this was well counterfeited! I pray
you tell your brother how well I counterfeited.
Heigh-ho!

Oliver   This was not counterfeit, there is too great
testimony in your complexion that it was a passion
171   of earnest.

Rosalind   Counterfeit, I assure you.

Oliver   Well then, take a good heart and counterfeit
to be a man.

Rosalind   So I do; but, i' faith, I should have been a
176   woman by right.

Celia   Come, you look paler and paler. Pray you
draw homewards. Good sir, go with us.

Oliver   That will I, for I must bear answer back
180   How you excuse my brother, Rosalind.

Rosalind   I shall devise something; but I pray you
commend my counterfeiting to him. Will you go?

Exeunt.

Rosalind   I do, I tell you. Really, fellow, anybody would think that my fainting was very convincing! Tell your brother, please, how well I faked it. Ha, ha!

Oliver   [*shaking his head skeptically*] That wasn't faked. The color of your complexion shows that it was from genuine emotion.

Rosalind   It was fake, I promise you.

Oliver: [*still unconvinced*] Well, then, take courage and pretend that you're a man.

Rosalind   [*shrugging*] I do, but really I should have been a woman.

Celia   [*to* **Rosalind**] Come, you're looking paler and paler. Please, let's head home.

[*to* **Oliver**] Kind sir, come with us.

Oliver   I will, but I must take an answer back to my brother saying that you forgive him, "Rosalind."

Rosalind   I'll think of something. But, please, be sure to tell him how well I faked fainting. Are you coming?

[*They all leave together,* **Celia** *and* **Oliver** *supporting* **Rosalind**.]

Act five

Scene 1

Enter Clown [**Touchstone**] *and* **Audrey**.

Touchstone   We shall find a time, Audrey, patience,
gentle Audrey.

Audrey   Faith, the priest was good enough, for all
4   the old gentleman's saying.

Touchstone   A most wicked Sir Oliver, Audrey, a most
vile Martext. But, Audrey, there is a youth here
in the forest lays claim to you.

Audrey   Ay, I know who 'tis; he hath no interest
in me in the world. Here comes the man you mean.

Enter **William**.

Touchstone   It is meat and drink to me to see a clown.
By my troth, we that have good wits have much to
12   answer for; we shall be flouting; we cannot hold.

William   Good ev'n, Audrey.

Audrey   God ye good ev'n, William.

15   **William**   And good ev'n to you, sir.

Act five

Scene 1

The Forest of Arden.

[**Touchstone** *and* **Audrey** *enter.*]

Touchstone   We'll find a time to marry, Audrey. Be patient, dear Audrey.

Audrey   Really, the priest was good enough, in spite of what Jaques said.

Touchstone   Sir Oliver Martext is wicked and disgusting. But, Audrey, there's a young man here in the forest who says you belong to him.

Audrey   Yes, I know who he is. He has no legal claim to me whatsoever. [*She sees* **William** *approaching.*] Here comes the fellow you mean.

Touchstone   [*chuckling in anticipation*] I love meeting a yokel. I swear, we intelligent folk ought to apologize; we're always making fun of fools. We can't help ourselves.
[*"Yokel" is an insulting term for a person who lives in the country, implying that the person is uneducated and lacks good manners.*]

[**William** *enters.*]

William   [*with awkward courtesy*] Good evening, Audrey.

Audrey   Good evening to you, William.

William   Good evening to you, sir.

Touchstone   Good ev'n, gentle friend. Cover thy head,
cover thy head; nay, prithee, be cover'd. How old
are you, friend?

William   Five and twenty, sir.

20 **Touchstone**   A ripe age. Is thy name William?

William   William, sir.

Touchstone   A fair name. Wast born i' the forest
here?

24 **William**   Ay, sir, I thank God.

Touchstone   "Thank God"—a good answer. Art rich?

William   Faith, sir, so, so.

Touchstone   "So, so" is good, very good, very excellent
good; and yet it is not, it is but so, so. Art thou wise?

29 **William**   Ay, sir, I have a pretty wit.

Touchstone   Why, thou say'st well. I do now remember a saying, "The fool doth think he is wise,
but the wise man knows himself to be a fool." The
heathen philosopher, when he had a desire to eat a
34 grape, would open his lips when he put it into
his mouth, meaning thereby that grapes were made
to eat and lips to open. You do love this maid?

William   I do, [sir].

Touchstone   Give me your hand. Art thou learned?

Touchstone Good evening, noble friend. [*In calling* **William** *"noble,"* **Touchstone** *is being ironic, in that* **William** *is a peasant.*] Put your hat back on, put it on. [**William** *has removed his hat out of respect for one of higher social rank than he.*] No, please, put it on. How old are you, friend?

William Twenty-five, sir.

Touchstone That's a good age to be. Is your name William?

William Yes, it's William, sir.

Touchstone That's a fine name. Were you born here in the forest?

William Yes, sir, thank God.

Touchstone "Thank God" is a good answer. Are you rich?

William Well, sir, so-so.

Touchstone "So-so" is a good answer, very good. In fact, an excellent answer. Yet, it isn't good because it's only "so-so." Are you wise?

William Yes, sir, I have a good mind.

Touchstone [*nodding judiciously*] Why, that's a good answer. I just remembered a saying: "The fool thinks he's wise, but the wise man knows he's a fool." When the pagan philosopher wanted to eat a grape, he would open his lips when he put it into his mouth, demonstrating by doing so that grapes were made to eat and lips to open. Do you love this girl? [**Touchstone's** *remark about the philosopher is a jibe at* **William** *who is staring in open-mouthed confusion over* **Touchstone's** *comments.*]

William I do, sir.

Touchstone Give me your hand. Are you highly educated?

233

39 **William**   No, sir.

Touchstone   Then learn this of me: to have, is to have.
For it is a figure in rhetoric that drink, being pour'd out
of a cup into a glass, by filling the one doth empty the
other. For all your writers do consent that *ipse* is he:
now, you are not *ipse*, for I am he.

45 **William**   Which he, sir?

Touchstone   He, sir, that must marry this woman.
Therefore, you clown, abandon—which is in the
vulgar leave—the society—which in the boorish is
49 company—of this female—which in the common
is woman; which together is, abandon the society of
this female, or, clown, thou perishest; or to thy better
understanding, diest; or (to wit) I kill thee, make thee
away, translate thy life into death, thy liberty into
bondage. I will deal in poison with thee, or in basti-
55 nado, or in steel; I will bandy with thee in faction; I
will o'errun thee with [policy]; I will kill thee a
hundred and fifty ways: therefore tremble and depart.

Audrey   Do, good William.

William   God rest you merry, sir.

Exit.

Enter **Corin**.

Corin   Our master and mistress seeks you. Come
61 away, away!

Touchstone   Trip, Audrey, trip, Audrey! I attend, I
attend.

Exeunt.

William   No, sir.

Touchstone   Then let me teach you. If you have something, you have it. In rhetoric, one says that when you pour a liquid from a cup into a glass, by filling one, you empty the other. All writers agree that "*ipse*" means "he"; you aren't *ipse* because I am he.

William   Which "he," sir?

Touchstone   The "he," sir, who is going to marry this woman. Therefore, you dummy, abandon (which in plain language means "leave")—the society (uneducated people would say "the company")—of this female (or, in ordinary words, "of this woman"). Put the words all together, and you have: "Abandon the society of this female," or, dummy, you will perish. To put it in a way that you will understand, you will die. In other words, I will kill you, get rid of you, transform your life to death, your freedom to captivity. I will poison you, or club you, or take a sword to you. I will argue with you until we become physically violent; I will defeat you with cunning; I will find one hundred fifty ways to kill you. Therefore, tremble with fear and go.

Audrey   [*awed at* **Touchstone's** *verbal display*] Do as he says, William.

William   God bless you, sir.

[**William**, *not knowing what to say, utters a common form of farewell and leaves.*]

[**Corin** *enters.*]

Corin   Our master and mistress are looking for you. Come, quickly! Quickly!

Touchstone   Hurry, Audrey, hurry! I'm coming; I'm coming.

[**Touchstone**, **Audrey**, *and* **Corin** *leave rapidly.*]

Scene 2

Enter **Orlando** *and* **Oliver**.

Orlando   Is't possible that on so little acquaintance
you should like her? that but seeing, you should
love her? and loving, woo? and wooing, she should
4   grant? and will you persever to enjoy her?

Oliver   Neither call the giddiness of it in question,
the poverty of her, the small acquaintance, my sudden
wooing, nor [her] sudden consenting; but say with me,
I love Aliena; say with her that she loves me; consent
with both that we may enjoy each other. It shall be
10   to your good; for my father's house and all the
revenue that was old Sir Rowland's will I estate upon
you, and here live and die a shepherd.

Enter **Rosalind**.

Orlando   You have my consent. Let your wedding
14   be to-morrow; thither will I invite the Duke and
all's contented followers. Go you and prepare Aliena;
for look you, here comes my Rosalind.

Rosalind   God save you, brother.

Oliver   And you, fair sister.

[*Exit.*]

Rosalind   O my dear Orlando, how it grieves me to
20   see thee wear thy heart in a scarf!

Scene 2

The Forest of Arden.

[**Orlando** *and* **Oliver** *enter.*]

Orlando   Is it possible that, hardly knowing Aliena, you should like her? That you should love her just by seeing her? And that, having fallen in love, you should woo her? And that she should respond to your wooing? And will you persist in wooing until you win her?

Oliver   Don't bother to question the suddenness of it all, or her poverty, or the short time we've known each other, or the speed of my wooing, or of her quick acceptance. Just accept what we say, that I love Aliena and she loves me. Support us in our plan to enjoy one another. You will benefit by doing so, for I will give you my father's house and all the income from his property, and I will live and die here as a shepherd.

Orlando   [*shaking his brother's hand heartily*] You have my consent. Your wedding will be tomorrow. I'll invite the duke and all of his happy followers to come. Go and tell Aliena, for, look, here comes my Rosalind.

[**Rosalind**, *dressed as* **Ganymede**, *enters.*]

Rosalind   [*speaking as* **Ganymede** *to* **Oliver**] Good day to you, brother.

Oliver   [*speaking to* **Ganymede** *as if "he" is* "**Rosalind**"] And to you, lovely sister.

[**Oliver** *leaves.*]

Rosalind   [*speaking melodramatically to cover her true feelings*] Oh, my dear Orlando, it deeply upsets me to see your heart covered with a bandage!

Orlando   It is my arm.

Rosalind   I thought thy heart had been wounded with the claws of a lion.

Orlando   Wounded it is, but with the eyes of a lady.

Rosalind   Did your brother tell you how I counterfeited to sound when he show'd me your handker-
27   cher?

Orlando   Ay, and greater wonders than that.

Rosalind   O, I know where you are. Nay, 'tis true.
There was never any thing so sudden but the fight of
two rams, and Caesar's thrasonical brag of "I came,
saw, and [overcame]." For your brother and my
sister no sooner met but they look'd; no sooner look'd
but they lov'd; no sooner lov'd but they sigh'd; no
35   sooner sigh'd but they ask'd one another the
reason; no sooner knew the reason but they sought the
remedy: and in these degrees have they made a pair
of stairs to marriage, which they will climb inconti-
39   nent, or else be incontinent before marriage. They
are in the very wrath of love, and they will together.
Clubs cannot part them.

Orlando   They shall be married to-morrow; and I
will bid the Duke to the nuptial. But O, how bitter
44   a thing it is to look into happiness through another
man's eyes! By so much the more shall I to-morrow be
at the height of heart-heaviness, by how much I shall
think my brother happy in having what he wishes for.

Rosalind   Why then to-morrow I cannot serve your
turn for Rosalind?

50 **Orlando**   I can live no longer by thinking.

Orlando [*startled*] It's my arm.

Rosalind I thought your heart had been wounded by a lion's claws.

Orlando It *is* wounded, but it was by a lady's eyes.

Rosalind Did your brother tell you how I pretended to faint when he showed me your handkerchief?

Orlando Yes, and even more amazing things than that.

Rosalind [*in sympathetic amusement*] Oh, I know what you're talking about. No, it's true. Nothing has ever been so sudden, other than two rams attacking one another or Caesar's ridiculous boast, "I came, I saw, I conquered." As soon as your brother and my sister met, they stared at one another; as soon as they stared, they fell in love; as soon as they loved, they sighed; as soon as they sighed, they asked one another why they did so; as soon as they knew why, they looked for the solution to their situation. And by these steps, they've made a flight of stairs to marriage, which they'll either climb very quickly or else they will be unable to wait until they are married to make love. They're madly in love and they must be together. You couldn't separate them if you beat them with clubs.

Orlando [*sighing heavily*] They're going to be married tomorrow, and I'll invite the duke to the wedding. But it's a bitter experience to only be allowed to look at happiness in another man's eyes. Tomorrow, my deep sadness will be even greater knowing how happy my brother is in having what he wants.

Rosalind So then tomorrow I will not be enough "Rosalind" for you?

Orlando [*shaking his head sadly*] I can no longer live by pretending.

Rosalind   I will weary you then no longer with idle
talking. Know of me then (for now I speak to some
purpose) that I know you are a gentleman of good
54   conceit. I speak not this that you should bear a
good opinion of my knowledge, insomuch I say I know
you are; neither do I labor for a greater esteem than
may in some little measure draw a belief from you, to
do yourself good, and not to grace me. Believe then, if
59   you please, that I can do strange things. I have,
since I was three year old, convers'd with a magician,
most profound in his art, and yet not damnable. If
you do love Rosalind so near the heart as your gesture
cries it out, when your brother marries Aliena, shall
64   you marry her. I know into what straits of fortune
she is driven, and it is not impossible to me, if it
appear not inconvenient to you, to set her before your
eyes to-morrow, human as she is, and without any
danger.

69 **Orlando**   Speak'st thou in sober meanings?

Rosalind   By my life I do, which I tender dearly,
though I say I am a magician. Therefore put you
in your best array, bid your friends; for if you will
be married to-morrow, you shall; and to Rosalind,
74   if you will.

Enter **Silvius** *and* **Phebe**.

Look, here comes a lover of mine and a lover of
hers.

Phebe   Youth, you have done me much ungentleness,
To show the letter that I writ to you.

Rosalind   [*decisively*] I won't wear you out any longer then with pointless talk. Learn from me then—I'm now speaking to you seriously—for I know you are an intelligent gentleman. I'm not trying to make you think I'm smart by telling you that I know *you're* smart. I'm also not trying to improve my reputation except for the purpose of helping you believe that I can do something to help you. Please believe then that I can do amazing things. Since I was three years old, I have spent time learning from a magician, a man who is very knowledgeable about magic—but not black magic. If you love Rosalind as much as your actions indicate, when your brother marries Aliena you shall marry Rosalind. I know what her situation is, and it isn't impossible for me, assuming that you don't think it somehow improper, to make her appear in human form—not just as some sort of phantom—before your eyes tomorrow.

Orlando   Are you serious?

Rosalind   I swear on my life, which I greatly value, even if I do admit to being a magician. Therefore, put on your best clothes and invite your friends because you will be married tomorrow—yes, you will—and to Rosalind, if that's what you want. [*Practicing magic was punishable by death and had the added risk of damnation because of involvement with evil spirits, so* **Rosalind's** *admission could have been very risky.*]

[**Silvius** *and* **Phebe** *enter.*]

Look, here comes a lover of mine and a lover of hers.

Phebe   [*with strong indignation*] Young man, you have been very unkind to me in showing Silvius the letter that I wrote to you.

Rosalind   I care not if I have. It is my study
80   To seem despiteful and ungentle to you.
You are there followed by a faithful shepherd—
Look upon him, love him; he worships you.

Phebe   Good shepherd, tell this youth what 'tis to
love.

Silvius   It is to be all made of sighs and tears,
85   And so am I for Phebe.

Phebe   And I for Ganymed.

Orlando   And I for Rosalind.

Rosalind   And I for no woman.

Silvius   It is to be all made of faith and service,
90   And so am I for Phebe.

Phebe   And I for Ganymed.

Orlando   And I for Rosalind.

Rosalind   And I for no woman.

Silvius   It is to be all made of fantasy,
95   All made of passion, and all made of wishes,
All adoration, duty, and observance,
All humbleness, all patience, and impatience,
All purity, all trial, all observance;
And so am I for Phebe.

100 **Phebe**   And so am I for Ganymed.

Orlando   And so am I for Rosalind.

Rosalind   And so am I for no woman.

Phebe   If this be so, why blame you me to love you?

Rosalind [*with cold impatience*] I don't care if I have. I've been hateful and unkind to you on purpose. This faithful shepherd wants you. Look at him. Love him. He worships you.

Phebe Good Silvius, tell this boy what it means to be in love.

Silvius [*sighing soulfully*] It means doing nothing but sighing and weeping, as I do for Phebe.

Phebe [*sighing soulfully*] As I do for Ganymede.

Orlando [*sighing soulfully*] As I do for Rosalind.

Rosalind But there is no woman who makes me sigh and weep.

Silvius [*earnestly*] Being in love is about being faithful and performing acts of devotion, as I do for Phebe.

Phebe As I do for Ganymede.

Orlando As I do for Rosalind.

Rosalind I don't do those things for any woman.

Silvius [*with adoring gaze*] It's like living in a dream world, filled with passion and longings, complete adoration, reverence, and devotion, total humility, patience and impatience, absolute purity, endurance, devotion. That's how I love Phebe.

Phebe [*with adoring gaze*] And how I love Ganymede.

Orlando [*with adoring gaze*] And how I love Rosalind.

Rosalind But that's not how I feel about any woman.

Phebe [*plaintively, to* **Ganymede**] If these things are true, why do you blame me for loving you?

Silvius   If this be so, why blame you me to love you?

Orlando   If this be so, why blame you me to love you?

Rosalind   Why do you speak too, "Why blame you
107   me to love you?"

Orlando   To her that is not here, nor doth not hear.

Rosalind   Pray you, no more of this, 'tis like the howling of Irish wolves against the moon. [*To* **Silvius**.] I
111   will help you if I can: [*To* **Phebe**.] I would love
you if I could.—To-morrow meet me all together.
[*To* **Phebe**.] I will marry you, if ever I marry woman,
and I'll be married to-morrow. [*To* **Orlando**.] I will
satisfy you, if ever I satisfied man, and you shall be
116   married to-morrow. [*To* **Silvius**.] I will content
you, if what pleases you contents you, and you
shall be married to-morrow. [*To* **Orlando**.] As you
love Rosalind, meet. [*To* **Silvius**.] As you love Phebe,
meet. And as I love no woman, I'll meet. So fare
121   you well; I have left you commands.

Silvius   I'll not fail, if I live.

Phebe   Nor I.

Orlando   Nor I.

Exeunt.

Silvius   [*plaintively, to* **Phebe**] If these things are true, why do you blame me for loving you?

Orlando   [*to* **Ganymede** *as* "**Rosalind**"] If these things are true, why do you blame me for loving you?

Rosalind   [*sharply*] Who are you speaking to when you say, "Why do you blame me for loving you?"

Orlando   To the woman who isn't here and can't hear me.

Rosalind   [*impatiently, to* **Silvius**, **Phebe**, *and* **Orlando**] Please, let's stop all this. You're like a pack of Irish wolves howling at the moon.

[*to* **Silvius**] I'll help you, if I can.

[*to* **Phebe**] I would love you, if I could.

[*to* **Silvius**, **Phebe**, *and* **Orlando**] Meet me here, all of you together, tomorrow.

[*to* **Phebe**] If I ever marry a woman—and I will be married tomorrow—I will marry you.

[*to* **Orlando**] I will satisfy you—if I ever satisfy a man—and you will be married tomorrow.

[*to* **Silvius**] I will give you what you want—if what you want will make you happy—and you will be married tomorrow.

[*to* **Orlando**] If you love Rosalind, be here.

[*to* **Silvius**] If you love Phebe, be here. And, I swear by the truth that I love no woman, I'll be here. So, goodbye. I've left you with your instructions.

Silvius   If I'm living, I'll be here.

Phebe   So will I.

Orlando   So will I.

[*They all leave.*]

Scene 3

Enter Clown [**Touchstone**] *and* **Audrey**.

Touchstone   To-morrow is the joyful day, Audrey, to-morrow will we be married.

Audrey   I do desire it with all my heart; and I hope it is no dishonest desire to desire to be a woman of the world. Here come two of the banish'd Duke's
6   pages.

Enter two **Pages**.

First Page   Well met, honest gentleman.

Touchstone   By my troth, well met. Come, sit, sit, and a song.

10 **Second Page**   We are for you, sit i' th' middle.

First Page   Shall we clap into't roundly, without hawking or spitting or saying we are hoarse, which are the only prologues to a bad voice?

Second Page   I' faith, i' faith, and both in a tune, like
15   two gipsies on a horse.

Scene 3

The Forest of Arden.

[**Touchstone** *and* **Audrey** *enter.*]

Touchstone   Tomorrow is the happy day, Audrey. Tomorrow we'll be married.

Audrey   I want it with all my heart. And I hope it's not slutty of me to want to be a married woman. Here come two of the banished duke's pages.

[*Two* **Pages** *enter.*]

First Page   Greetings, good gentleman.

Touchstone   Greetings to you. Come, sit, sit, and sing a song.

Second Page   Gladly. Sit between us.

First Page   Shall we start right away, without hacking or spitting or saying we're hoarse, which bad singers do to excuse their singing?

Second Page   Yes, yes, and we'll sing in unison, like two gypsies riding on one horse.

SONG

It was a lover and his lass,
   With a hey, and a ho, and a hey nonino,
That o'er the green corn-field did pass,
   In spring time, the only pretty [ring]
      time,
20   When birds do sing, hey ding a ding, ding,
Sweet lovers love the spring.

Between the acres of the rye,
   With a hey, and a ho, and a hey nonino,
These pretty country folks would lie,
25   In spring time, etc.

This carol they began that hour,
   With a hey, and a ho, and a hey nonino,
How that a life was but a flower,
    In spring time, etc.

30   And therefore take the present time,
   With a hey, and a ho, and a hey nonino,
For love is crowned with the prime,
    In spring time, etc.

Touchstone   Truly, young gentlemen, though there
was no great matter in the ditty, yet the note was
36 very untuneable.

First Page   You are deceiv'd, sir, we kept time, we
lost not our time.

First and **Second Pages**   [*singing*]

> There was a lover and his girl,
> With a "hey," and a "ho," and a "hey nonino,"
> Who walked across the green wheat field
> In the springtime, the best wedding ring time,
> The time when birds sing, hey, ding a ding, ding.
> Sweet lovers love the spring.
>
> In the grassy borders between fields of rye,
> With a "hey," and a "ho," and a "hey nonino,"
> These pretty country folks would lie,
> In the springtime, the best wedding ring time,
> The time when birds sing, hey, ding a ding, ding.
> Sweet lovers love the spring.
>
> They began to sing that very hour,
> With a "hey," and a "ho," and a "hey nonino,"
> Saying that life is as brief as a flower.
> In the springtime, the best wedding ring time,
> The time when birds sing, hey, ding a ding, ding.
> Sweet lovers love the spring.
>
> And therefore seize this present time,
> With a "hey," and a "ho," and a "hey nonino,"
> For in the spring love is the king.
> In the springtime, the best wedding ring time,
> The time when birds sing, hey, ding a ding, ding.
> Sweet lovers love the spring.

Touchstone   [*applauding*] Really, young gentlemen, even though the content of the song wasn't much, at least it was out of tune.

First Page   [*indignantly*] You're wrong, sir! We kept the rhythm; we didn't lose the time.

Touchstone   By my troth, yes; I count it but time lost
to hear such a foolish song. God buy you, and God
41   mend your voices! Come, Audrey.

Exeunt.

Scene 4

Enter **Duke Senior**, **Amiens**, **Jaques**, **Orlando**,
Oliver, **Celia**.

Duke Senior   Dost thou believe, Orlando, that the boy
Can do all this that he hath promised?

Orlando   I sometimes do believe, and sometimes do not,
As those that fear they hope, and know they fear.

Enter **Rosalind**, **Silvius**, *and* **Phebe**.

Rosalind   Patience once more, whiles our compact is
5   urg'd:
You say, if I bring in your Rosalind,
You will bestow her on Orlando here?

Duke Senior   That would I, had I kingdoms to give
with her.

Rosalind   And you say you will have her, when I
9   bring her.

Touchstone   Oh, yes, in fact, time was lost because it's a waste of time to listen to such a stupid song. Goodbye, and may God improve your voices.

[*to* **Audrey**] Let's go, Audrey.

[**Touchstone** *and* **Audrey** *leave in one direction, while the* **Pages** *stalk off another way.*]

Scene 4

The Forest of Arden.

[**Duke Senior**, **Amiens**, **Jaques**, **Orlando**, **Oliver** *and* **Celia** *as* **Aliena** *enter.*]

Duke Senior   Do you believe, Orlando, that the boy can do everything that he has promised to do?

Orlando   Sometimes I do believe it and sometimes I don't. I'm like those who fear that they're only hoping, but I do know that I'm afraid of being disappointed.

[**Rosalind** *as* **Ganymede**, **Silvius**, *and* **Phebe** *enter.*]

Rosalind   [*to all present*] Please be patient while we spell out the terms of our agreement.

[*to* **Duke Senior**] You say that, if I present your Rosalind, you will give her in marriage to Orlando here?

Duke Senior   I certainly would, even if I had kingdoms to give with her.

Rosalind   [*to* **Orlando**] And you say that you will marry her when I bring her?

Orlando   That would I, were I of all kingdoms king.

Rosalind   You say you'll marry me, if I be willing?

Phebe   That will I, should I die the hour after.

Rosalind   But if you do refuse to marry me,
You'll give yourself to this most faithful shepherd?

15 **Phebe**   So is the bargain.

Rosalind   You say that you'll have Phebe, if she will?

Silvius   Though to have her and death were both one
thing.

Rosalind   I have promis'd to make all this matter even:
Keep you your word, O Duke, to give your daughter;
20   You, yours, Orlando, to receive his daughter;
Keep you your word, Phebe, that you'll marry me,
Or else, refusing me, to wed this shepherd;
Keep your word, Silvius, that you'll marry her
If she refuse me; and from hence I go
25   To make these doubts all even.

Exeunt **Rosalind** *and* **Celia**.

Duke Senior   I do remember in this shepherd boy
Some lively touches of my daughter's favor.

Orlando   I certainly would, even if I were a king of all kingdoms.

Rosalind   [*to* **Phebe**] And you will marry me if I'm willing?

Phebe   [*nodding emphatically*] I certainly will, even if I die an hour later.

Rosalind   [*sternly*] But if you refuse to marry me, will you marry this faithful shepherd instead?

Phebe   [*gazing starry-eyed at* "**Ganymede**"] That's our bargain.

Rosalind   [*to* **Silvius**] And will you marry Phebe, if she's willing?

Silvius   Even if I had to die to marry her.

Rosalind   I've promised to straighten everything out.

[*to* **Duke Senior**] You, Duke, must keep your promise to let your daughter marry.

[*to* **Orlando**] You, Orlando, must keep yours to marry his daughter.

[*to* **Phebe**] You, Phebe, keep your promise to marry me, or if you decide to refuse me, to marry this shepherd.

[*to* **Silvius**] And you, Silvius, keep your promise that you'll marry her if she refuses to marry me.

[*to all present*] I'm leaving now to put an end to all your doubts.

[**Rosalind** *and* **Celia** *leave.*]

Duke Senior   [*thoughtfully*] It seems to me that this shepherd boy looks a lot like my daughter.

Orlando   My lord, the first time that I ever saw him
Methought he was a brother to your daughter.
30   But, my good lord, this boy is forest-born,
And hath been tutor'd in the rudiments
Of many desperate studies by his uncle,
Whom he reports to be a great magician,
34   Obscured in the circle of this forest.

Enter Clown [**Touchstone**] *and* **Audrey**.

Jaques   There is sure another flood toward, and
these couples are coming to the ark. Here comes a
pair of very strange beasts, which in all tongues are
call'd fools.

39 **Touchstone**   Salutation and greeting to you all!

Jaques   Good my lord, bid him welcome. This is
the motley-minded gentleman that I have so often
met in the forest. He hath been a courtier, he swears.

Touchstone   If any man doubt that, let him put me to my
44   purgation. I have trod a measure; I have flatt'red a
lady, I have been politic with my friend, smooth with
mine enemy, I have undone three tailors, I have had
four quarrels, and like to have fought one.

Jaques   And how was that ta'en up?

Touchstone   Faith, we met, and found the quarrel was
50   upon the seventh cause.

Orlando My Lord, the first time I saw him, I thought he was your daughter's brother. But, My Lord, this boy was born in the forest and has been instructed in the basics of many dangerous supernatural practices by his uncle, who he says is a great magician, living in hiding within the forest.

[**Touchstone** *and* **Audrey** *enter.*]

Jaques There must certainly be another great flood coming, and these couples are coming to get on Noah's ark. Here comes a pair of strange animals, which in any language would be called "fools." [*In Genesis, God told Noah to build a large boat (an ark) and fill it with pairs of beasts of all kinds before God sent a flood to destroy all living things that were not in the ark.*]

Touchstone Hello, and greetings to you all!

Jaques [*to* **Duke Senior**] My Lord, welcome him. This is the fascinating jester that I have met so often in the forest. He swears that he has been a member of the court.

Touchstone If anyone doubts it, let him test me. I know how to do the formal dances, I can flatter a lady, I have been diplomatic with my friend and put on a false show of courtesy with my enemy. I have ruined three tailors by not paying them, I've had four formal disputes, and I nearly fought a duel over one of them.

Jaques And how was that one settled?

Touchstone Well, we were ready to duel, but we discovered that our disagreement was for "the seventh cause."

Jaques   How seventh cause? Good my lord, like
this fellow.

Duke Senior   I like him very well.

Touchstone   God 'ild you, sir, I desire you of the like.
55   I press in here, sir, amongst the rest of the country
copulatives, to swear and to forswear, according as
marriage binds and blood breaks. A poor virgin, sir, an
ill-favor'd thing, sir, but mine own; a poor humor of
59   mine, sir, to take that that no man else will. Rich
honesty dwells like a miser, sir, in a poor house, as
your pearl in your foul oyster.

Duke Senior   By my faith, he is very swift and sen-
tentious.

Touchstone   According to the fool's bolt, sir, and such
65   dulcet diseases.

Jaques   But for the seventh cause—how did you find
the quarrel on the seventh cause?

Jaques   What do you mean by "the seventh cause"?

[*to* **Duke Senior**] My Lord, I hope you like this fellow.

Duke Senior   [*with eyes twinkling at* **Touchstone's** *remarks*] I like him very well.

Touchstone   [*bowing formally to the duke*] May God bless you, sir, and I hope you wish me the same. I have pushed myself in here, sir, in the midst of all the rest of these country folk who want to be married, in order to commit myself in marriage and to give up any other women, as the marriage vows require and in spite of any lusts that may make it difficult to be faithful. She's a poor virgin, sir, and ugly, sir, but she's all mine. It's just a whim of mine, sir, to take what no other man wants. Her sexual purity is like a rich man living in poverty, sir, in a humble house; it's like the pearl you find in an ugly oyster.

Duke Senior   [*to* **Jaques**] My word, he's very quick-witted and full of clever sayings!

Touchstone   Like other fools, I'm quick to let my "arrows" fly, sir, and sometimes they even hit their target.

Jaques   But what about "the seventh cause"? Why do you say that the quarrel was based on the seventh cause?

Touchstone   Upon a lie seven times remov'd (bear your
body more seeming, Audrey), as thus, sir. I did dis-
70   like the cut of a certain courtier's beard. He sent
me word, if I said his beard was not cut well, he was in
the mind it was: this is call'd the Retort Courteous.
If I sent him word again, it was not well cut, he
would send me word he cut it to please himself: this
is call'd the Quip Modest. If again, it was not well
76   cut, he disabled my judgment: this is call'd the
Reply Churlish. If again, it was not well cut, he
would answer I spake not true: this is call'd the
Reproof Valiant. If again, it was not well cut, he
80   would say I lie: this is call'd the Countercheck
Quarrelsome; and so to Lie Circumstantial and the Lie
Direct.

Jaques   And how oft did you say his beard was not
84   well cut?

Touchstone   It was all based on a lie that had gone through seven stages—

[*to* **Audrey**, *who is standing awkwardly*] Don't stand like that, Audrey.

[*to* **Duke Senior** *and* **Jaques**] It was like this, sir. I criticized the style of a certain courtier's beard. He sent me word that, even though I had said his beard was poorly cut, he believed that it was cut well. This is called "The Polite Response." If I sent him another message that it wasn't cut well, he would send me a message saying that he cut it the way he liked it. This is called "The Sarcastic Answer." If I again said that it wasn't cut well, he would say I had bad taste. This is called "The Rude Reply." If I said it again, he would answer that I was not correct; this is called "The Brave Rebuke." If I said it again, he would say I was lying; this is called "The Quarrelsome Contradiction." And so on, until we had reached "The Circumstantial Lie" and "The Intentional Lie." [*"The Circumstantial Lie" meant that the other person was saying that* **Touchstone** *was lying, but not intentionally; "The Intentional Lie" meant that* **Touchstone** *was a liar, a deliberate insult.*]

Jaques   And how many times did you say that his beard was not cut well?

Touchstone   I durst go no further than the Lie Circumstantial, nor he durst not give me the Lie Direct;
and so we measur'd swords and parted.

Jaques   Can you nominate in order now the degrees
89   of the lie?

Touchstone   O sir, we quarrel in print, by the book—
as you have books for good manners. I will name you
the degrees. The first, the Retort Courteous; the
second, the Quip Modest; the third, the Reply
94   Churlish; the fourth, the Reproof Valiant; the
fift, the Countercheck Quarrelsome; the sixt, the
Lie with Circumstance; the seventh, the Lie Direct.
All these you may avoid but the Lie Direct; and you
may avoid that too, with an If. I knew when seven
99   justices could not take up a quarrel, but when the
parties were met themselves, one of them thought but
of an If, as, "If you said so, then I said so"; and they
shook hands and swore brothers. Your If is the only
peacemaker; much virtue in If.

Jaques   Is not this a rare fellow, my lord? He's as
105   good at any thing, and yet a fool.

Duke Senior   He uses his folly like a stalking-horse,
and under the presentation of that he shoots his wit.

Enter **Hymen**, **Rosalind**, *and* **Celia**. *Still Music.*

Touchstone   I didn't dare go past "The Circumstantial Lie," and he didn't dare call me a liar, so we compared the lengths of our swords, and then we went home. [*When people dueled with swords, the swords' lengths were compared to make sure they were the same so that neither fighter would have an unfair advantage in having a longer weapon.* **Touchstone** *means that he and his opponent pretended that their swords weren't the same length to give them an excuse not to fight.*]

Jaques   Can you list the different levels of a lie in order?

Touchstone   Oh, sir, we argue properly, in accordance with the rule books, in the same way that you have etiquette books. I'll list the degrees for you. First, there's "The Polite Response"; second, "The Sarcastic Answer"; third, "The Rude Reply"; fourth, "The Brave Rebuke"; fifth, "The Quarrelsome Contradiction"; sixth, "The Circumstantial Lie"; and seventh, "The Intentional Lie." It's possible to get out of all of these except "The Intentional Lie," and you may avoid that one, too, by saying, "If." I knew of a case in which seven judges were unable to settle a quarrel, but when the people involved talked it over, one of them thought of an "if," saying, "If you said this, then I said that." So they shook hands and swore to treat one another like loving brothers. "If" is an exceptional peacemaker; "if" is a very good word. [**Touchstone's** *list is intended as a parody of actual books concerning the code of conduct for dueling.*]

Jaques   [*to* **Duke Senior**] Isn't this fellow amazing, My Lord? He's very clever, yet he's a fool.

Duke Senior   He uses his appearance of foolishness to sneak up on people and fire off his wit at them.

[**Hymen**, *the god of marriage, with* **Rosalind** *and* **Celia**, *dressed as themselves, enter to soft music.*]

Hymen   Then is there mirth in heaven,
When earthly things made even
110   Atone together.
Good Duke, receive thy daughter,
Hymen from heaven brought her,
            Yea, brought her hither,
That thou mightst join [her] hand with his
115   Whose heart within his bosom is.

Rosalind   [*To* **Duke Senior**.] To you I give myself, for I
am yours.
[*To* **Orlando**.] To you I give myself, for I am yours.

Duke Senior   If there be truth in sight, you are my
daughter.

Orlando   If there be truth in sight, you are my Rosalind.

120 **Phebe**   If sight and shape be true,
Why then my love adieu!

Rosalind   I'll have no father, if you be not he;
I'll have no husband, if you be not he;
Nor ne'er wed woman, if you be not she.

Hymen   There is joy in heaven when things on earth come together in harmony.

[*to* **Duke Senior**] Good duke, here is your daughter. Hymen has brought her, yes, brought her here from heaven so that you could join her hand in marriage with the man to whom her heart already belongs.

Rosalind   [*to* **Duke Senior**] I give myself to you, for I am yours.

[*to* **Orlando**] I give myself to you, for I am yours.

Duke Senior   If my eyes are not deceiving me, you are my daughter.

Orlando   [*joyfully*] If my eyes are not deceiving me, you are my Rosalind.

Phebe   [*glumly*] If what I'm seeing is true, then it's goodbye to my love.

Rosalind   [*solemnly, as one reciting marriage vows, first to* **Duke Senior**] If you are not my father, I'll have no father at all.

[*to* **Orlando**] If you are not my husband, I'll have no husband at all.

[*to* **Phebe**] Nor will I marry any woman, if I don't marry you.

125 **Hymen**   Peace ho! I bar confusion,
              'Tis I must make conclusion
                  Of these most strange events.
              Here's eight that must take hands
              To join in Hymen's bands,
130   If truth holds true contents.
[*To* **Orlando** and **Rosalind**.]
              You and you no cross shall part;
[*To* **Oliver** and **Celia**.]
              You and you are heart in heart;
[*To* **Phebe**.]
              You to his love must accord,
              Or have a woman to your lord;
[*To* **Touchstone** and **Audrey**.]
135   You and you are sure together,
              As the winter to foul weather.—
              Whiles a wedlock-hymn we sing,
              Feed yourselves with questioning;
              That reason wonder may diminish
              How thus we met, and these things finish.

SONG

141   Wedding is great Juno's crown,
                  O blessed bond of board and bed!
              'Tis Hymen peoples every town,
                  High wedlock then be honored.
145   Honor, high honor, and renown
              To Hymen, god of every town!

Duke Senior   O my dear niece, welcome thou art to me,
Even daughter, welcome, in no less degree.

Phebe   I will not eat my word, now thou art mine,
150 Thy faith my fancy to thee doth combine.

Enter Second Brother [**Jaques de Boys**].

264

Hymen [*sternly*] Silence! I forbid confusion. I will be the one to settle all these strange happenings. There are eight people here who must join hands to be married, if, now that the truth is known, it brings true happiness.

[*to* **Rosalind** *and* **Orlando**] No quarrel shall ever separate you.

[*to* **Celia** *and* **Oliver**] You have given your hearts to one another.

[*to* **Phebe**] You must accept Silvius' love or else you will have to marry a woman.

[*to* **Audrey** *and* **Touchstone**] You two go together like winter and bad weather.

[*to all the couples*] While we sing a wedding hymn, satisfy your curiosity by discussing how we came here today and how everything has ended as it has, so that your understanding may decrease your amazement.

> [*singing*] *Marriage is the crown of Juno;*
> *How blessed are the bonds of matrimony!*
> *Hymen fills the towns with people;*
> *Let marriage then be held in honor.*
> *Give honor, high honor, and esteem*
> *To Hymen, the god of every town!*
> [*Juno was the Roman goddess of marriage.*]

Duke Senior [*to* **Celia**, *embracing her*] Oh, my dear niece, I'm so glad to see you! You're as welcome here as if you were my daughter.

Phebe [*to* **Silvius**] I won't go back on my promise; your faithfulness has made me love you.

[**Jaques de Boys**, *middle son of Sir Rowland de Boys, enters.*]

Act five   Scene 4

Jaques de Boys   Let me have audience for a word or two.
I am the second son of old Sir Rowland,
That bring these tidings to this fair assembly.
Duke Frederick, hearing how that every day
155   Men of great worth resorted to this forest,
Address'd a mighty power, which were on foot
In his own conduct, purposely to take
His brother here, and put him to the sword;
And to the skirts of this wild wood he came;
160   Where, meeting with an old religious man,
After some question with him, was converted
Both from his enterprise and from the world,
His crown bequeathing to his banish'd brother,
And all their lands restor'd to [them] again
165   That were with him exil'd. This to be true,
I do engage my life.

Duke Senior   Welcome, young man;
Thou offer'st fairly to thy brothers' wedding:
To one his lands withheld, and to the other
A land itself at large, a potent dukedom.
170   First, in this forest let us do those ends
That here were well begun and well begot;
And after, every of this happy number,
That have endur'd shrewd days and nights with us,
Shall share the good of our returned fortune,
175   According to the measure of their states.
Mean time, forget this new-fall'n dignity,
And fall into our rustic revelry.
Play, music, and you brides and bridegrooms all,
With measure heap'd in joy, to th' measures fall.

Jaques   Sir, by your patience.—If I heard you rightly,
181   The Duke hath put on a religious life,
And thrown into neglect the pompous court?

266

Jaques de Boys   [*to all present*] Please let me have your attention for a moment. I'm the second son of old Sir Rowland, and I bring news to this fine group. Duke Frederick, hearing that each day high-ranking men were coming to the forest, had raised a large army which, under his command, was heading this way intent upon arresting Duke Senior, his brother, and killing him. He came to the outskirts of this wild forest, where he met an old religious man. After having some discussion with him, Duke Frederick gave up his plan and renounced all worldly things, giving his crown to Duke Senior, his banished brother. He also restored all the confiscated property to those who had been exiled with him. This, I swear it, is the truth.

Duke Senior   Welcome, young man! You bring excellent gifts to your brothers' wedding. To Oliver, you restore his confiscated lands, and to Orlando, an entire kingdom, a powerful dukedom. [**Duke Senior's** *kingdom has been restored to him, and therefore* **Orlando** *will be the next duke because of his marriage to* **Rosalind**.]

[*to all present*] But first, let's finish what we came here to do and have joyfully begun. Afterward, all those in this happy group who have suffered harsh days and nights with us shall be rewarded out of our good fortune, in proportion to their ranks. Meanwhile, let's forget about this newly acquired status and throw ourselves into these country festivities.

[*to musicians*] Play music!

[*to the couples*] And all you brides and grooms, dance to celebrate your marriage with overflowing joy.

Jaques   Sir, may I speak?

[*to* **Jaques de Boys**] Did I understand you correctly? The duke has become a monk and abandoned the ceremonious life at court?

Jaques de Boys   He hath.

Jaques   To him will I. Out of these convertites
185   There is much matter to be heard and learn'd.
         [*To* **Duke Senior**.] You to your former honor I be-
            queath,
         Your patience and your virtue well deserves it;
         [*To* **Orlando**.] You to a love that your true faith doth
            merit;
         [*To* **Oliver**.] You to your land, and love, and great
189   allies;
         [*To* **Silvius**.] You to a long and well-deserved bed;
         [*To* **Touchstone**.] And you to wrangling, for thy loving
            voyage
         Is but for two months victuall'd.—So to your pleas-
            ures,
         I am for other than for dancing measures.

194 **Duke Senior**   Stay, Jaques, stay.

     Jaques   To see no pastime I. What you would have
     I'll stay to know at your abandon'd cave.

                                                    Exit.

     Duke Senior   Proceed, proceed. We will begin these rites,
     As we do trust they'll end, in true delights.

                     [*A dance.*] *Exeunt* [*all but* **Rosalind**].

Jaques de Boys   He has.

Jaques   I'll go to him. One may learn a great deal from these religious converts.

[*to* **Duke Senior**] To you I leave your former rank; you deserve it because of your patience and goodness.

[*to* **Orlando**] To you I leave a love that your true love deserves.

[*to* **Oliver**] To you I leave your land and your love and strong allies.

[*to* **Silvius**] To you I leave a long and well-deserved sex life.

[*to* **Touchstone**] And to you I leave quarreling because your love is going to run out in two months.

[*to all*] So go back to celebrating. I will be dancing to a different tune. [**Jaques** *speaks metaphorically, meaning that he has other plans.*]

Duke Senior   Wait, Jaques, wait.

Jaques   I have no desire to celebrate. I'll wait at your abandoned cave to hear what you have to say.

[**Jaques** *leaves.*]

Duke Senior   Go on! Go on! We'll begin these marriages as we hope to see them end, in genuine happiness.

[*All join in a dance as they exit the stage, leaving only* **Rosalind** *behind.*]

[EPILOGUE]

Rosalind   It is not the fashion to see the lady the
epilogue; but it is no more unhandsome than to
see the lord the prologue. If it be true that good
wine needs no bush, 'tis true that a good play needs
5   no epilogue. Yet to good wine they do use good
bushes; and good plays prove the better by the help
of good epilogues. What a case am I in then, that
am neither a good epilogue, nor cannot insinuate
with you in the behalf of a good play! I am not
10   furnish'd like a beggar, therefore to beg will not
become me. My way is to conjure you, and I'll
begin with the women. I charge you, O women,
for the love you bear to men, to like as much of
this play as please you; and I charge you, O men,
15   for the love you bear to women (as I perceive
by your simp'ring, none of you hates them), that
between you and the women the play may please.
If I were a woman I would kiss as many of you as
had beards that pleas'd me, complexions that lik'd
20   me, and breaths that I defied not; and I am
sure, as many as have good beards, or good faces, or
sweet breaths, will for my kind offer, when I make
curtsy, bid me farewell.

Exit.

Rosalind   The heroine doesn't usually deliver the epilogue, but it's no more improper than having a man say the prologue. If it's true that people can tell a good wine even if the maker doesn't have a fancy sign with an ivy bush on it, then it's also true that a good play doesn't need an epilogue. But good wines *are* often advertised with effective signs, and good plays can be made even better with the help of good epilogues. So what a dilemma I'm in then that I don't have a good epilogue, and I can't win your good opinion on the play's behalf! I'm not dressed like a beggar, so it wouldn't be right for me to beg you. Instead, I will cast a spell on you, and I'll begin with the women. I command you, women, because you love men, to like the parts of this play that you enjoyed. And I command you, men, because you love women—as I can see by your smirking that you don't hate them—may the play bring pleasure to both of you. If I were a woman, I would kiss all of you whose beards I like, who have handsome faces, and whose breath doesn't disgust me. And I'm sure that all of you who have good beards or good faces or fresh breath will, when I make my final curtsy, in gratitude for my kind offer, bid me farewell. [*When* **Rosalind** *says that she is casting a spell on her audience, she does not intend for them to take her seriously, nor will they do so. When she says, "If I were a woman," the audience knew that the women's roles were played by boys dressed as women because acting was not considered to be a respectable occupation for women at that time.*]

[**Rosalind** *curtseys and leaves.*]

Activities

Structure

Pastoral Literature

At the time that Shakespeare wrote *As You Like It,* many literary works depicted a highly romanticized view of living in the country among shepherds and other farm workers; poems, stories, and plays containing these elements are referred to as "pastoral literature." Looked at from a structural perspective, pastoral literature involves a journey in which the main character must travel from the hectic and flawed world of civilization to the peaceful and innocent rural world. Within the rural world, he or she will travel to or encounter a supernatural world. While in the supernatural world, the main character resolves his or her "internal conflicts" and consequently is prepared to return to the outermost world of civilization. The changes in the main character may result as "a supernatural gift of a god, but sometimes the illumination is gained more painfully" (Wells Slights 20–21).

- Which of the locations in *As You Like It* correspond to those of pastoral literature?
- List all of the characters in the play who make a journey such as the one described above.
- Select one character who has made such a journey and explain how his or her journey corresponds to the elements described. Be sure to discuss what lesson he or she has learned and *why* the lesson needed to be learned by that character.
- How does Shakespeare incorporate the "supernatural world" in the play? Is the supernatural aspect of the play presented as being believable? Why or why not?

- In what ways does Shakespeare undermine the concept of the pastoral world as being a place of pure peace and innocence? Why does he do so?
- Oftentimes, pastoral literature features the passionate love of a shepherd for a shepherdess who rejects him. Which characters in the play correspond to the shepherd and shepherdess? Does Shakespeare present them in such a way as to cause us to like and sympathize with them or not? Explain your answer and support it with evidence from the play.
- Compare and contrast the shepherd and shepherdess to the other couples in the play. What do you think Shakespeare was trying to say about love by including the different relationships of the couples in the play?
- In pastoral literature, the "green world" (that is, the rural world) is typically depicted as being an idyllic place in which there are no problems. Does Shakespeare present the Forest of Arden and its surrounding countryside setting in this way? Why do you think he depicts the rural world as he does?

Robin Hood Games

From about 1400 to 1600, "Robin Hood games" were played throughout the summer in the villages of England, reenacting the stories associated with the famous outlaw and his band of "merry men." These games or plays had three main parts:

1 A person dressed as Robin Hood, along with his band of men, entered the village and set up a bower (an enclosure made out of vines or leafy braches), which represented Robin's "throne room" in the forest.
2 Some sort of sporting contest was acted out, such as the famous archery contest in which Little John and Friar Tuck compete, are captured by the Sheriff of Nottingham, and then are rescued by Robin Hood.

3   A feast—including drinking, dancing, eating, and singing—
    was held as a "communal celebration" (Leach 396).

Compare what happens in *As You Like It* to the Robin Hood
games. What events and characters in the play correspond to the
parts of the games listed above? Why did Shakespeare include
elements that are similar to the Robin Hood games? Based on
what happens in the play, do you think he was trying to send a
message about the political structures of his time? If so, what
was that message?

Allegory

Some of Shakespeare's plays have plots that are similar to the
allegorical dramas popular during the Middle Ages. An allegory
is a complete narrative that can be symbolically applied to other
circumstances, such as moral, political, or philosophical situations. Often, the characters in allegories personify abstract con-
cepts such as Vice, Lust, Good Deeds, or Pride.

Because *As You Like It* has certain elements that are similar to
things found in the Bible, some people think that Shakespeare
may have intended it to be an allegory. For example, the name
of Orlando's servant is Adam, which, according to the Bible, was
the name of the first man. Also, Oliver, Orlando's brother, is
attacked by a serpent, which brings to mind the temptation of
Eve by the serpent in the Garden of Eden.

- What other aspects of *As You Like It* are similar to people
  or things found in the Bible?
- Do you think the characters are intended to be repre-
  sentations of specific things such as Vice, Lust, Pride, or
  of some other abstract concept?
- Do you think that Shakespeare did intend this play to be
  an allegory? What are your reasons for thinking so?
- To what other situation or idea do you think the elements
  of this play can be applied?

Characters

Search the text to find answers to the following questions. They will help you to form opinions about the principle characters in the play. Record any relevant quotations in Shakespeare's own words.

Rosalind

Rosalind is the central character in *As You Like It*, and as Shakespearean expert Harold Bloom observes, "Rosalind is the most admirable personage in all Shakespeare" (207).

1 Make a list of the "admirable" qualities you see in Rosalind. Find evidence in the play of things that she says or does that support your ideas.

   a What qualities that are traditionally associated with being feminine does Rosalind demonstrate in what she says and does?

   b What qualities that are traditionally associated with being masculine does Rosalind demonstrate in what she says and does?

   c Do you think Shakespeare intended to say something about traditional roles of men and women through his depiction of Rosalind? Explain your reasons for your opinion.

2 When Rosalind is banished from the court of Duke Frederick, Celia says that they are going to "liberty, and not to banishment" (Act 1 Scene 3 line 138).

   a What are the various kinds of freedom that Rosalind enjoys in the Forest of Arden that she would not otherwise have been able to experience?

b To what extent does her disguise as Ganymede free her from social restrictions? How does Shakespeare enable her to take advantage of her freedom?

c To what extent does her disguise prevent her from doing what she wants to do? How does she overcome the difficulties presented by her false identity?

3 Rosalind expresses strong opinions on the subject of love.

a What is Rosalind's attitude toward love? Find lines in the play to support your opinion.

b Do her actions support or undermine what she says about love? Explain why you think so.

c Rosalind takes on the task, while still disguised as Ganymede, of teaching Orlando what it means to be in love. What does she manage to teach Orlando about love? Does her disguise as Ganymede make it easier or harder for her to teach him about love? Explain why you think so.

d Although Rosalind teaches others about love, are there any lessons about love that she must learn? If so, what are these lessons and how is she changed as a result of learning them?

4 On several occasions, Rosalind, in her disguise as Ganymede, cautions Orlando that Rosalind will be sexually unfaithful to him after they are married.

a Do you think that Rosalind really intends to cheat on Orlando after they are married? Why does she bring up the subject?

b Can you think of any other marital issues that Rosalind cautions Orlando about? What are they? Why does she tell him these things?

5 At times, Rosalind is critical of the actions or attitudes of other characters in the play.

  a Which characters does she criticize and for what reasons? What effect, if any, do her criticisms have on others? Do they cause them to change or not?

  b Does she ever criticize herself? If so, what are the things that she criticizes?

Orlando

Orlando, the youngest son of Sir Rowland de Boys, is the hero of the play.

1 When they meet before Orlando's wrestling match with Charles, Orlando and Rosalind fall in love at first sight.

  a What character traits does Orlando possess that would cause Rosalind to be attracted to him?

  b What other attributes does he have that would appeal to her?

2 When Rosalind gives Orlando the gift of a chain, he berates himself for being tongue-tied in her presence.

  a What do his actions in this scene indicate that he needs to learn?

  b Does he learn a lesson in this regard by the end of the play? What makes you think so?

3 Orlando demonstrates that he has ideas about love based on what is known as "courtly love." The conventions of courtly love demanded that the man must perform heroic acts in order to be worthy of the woman he loved, whom he idolized.

  a What aspects of the way Orlando behaves regarding his love for Rosalind demonstrate that his notions of love are based on the above definition?

b Does the poetry that Orlando writes demonstrate the ideals of courtly love? What are your reasons for your opinion?

c How does Rosalind react to the things Orlando does to show his love for her? How can you tell?

4 As a poor young gentleman, Orlando would not, under the social rules of the time, have had any hope of marrying Rosalind, who is a princess.

a How does Shakespeare show us that Orlando is worthy to be the husband of a princess?

b What situations or plot complications have to be overcome in order to permit them to marry? To what extent are they overcome as a result of something that Orlando does? Are any of the events that remove obstacles to Orlando's ability to marry Rosalind unrelated to what he does?

Jaques

Jaques is a nobleman who, like other members of Duke Senior's court, has followed the usurped duke into exile.

1 Make a list of words that you think describe Jaques.

a Which of the words you have written down are character traits (that is, aspects of his personality)? Cross out any words that are not character traits and then divide the remaining words into positive and negative character traits. Generally speaking, do you see Jaques as a positive or negative character?

b To what extent does your view of Jaques coincide with what he seems to think of himself?

c What do the other characters in the play think of him? Do you agree with their opinion or not?

2   In Act 2 Scene 1 lines 25–43 and 45–63, the First Lord describes Jaques' melancholy reaction to the dying deer.

   a Does the First Lord tell his story about Jaques in such a way as to indicate that he agrees with Jaques' response or not? Why do you think so?

   b Compare and contrast Duke Senior's thoughts about killing the deer (Act 2 Scene 1 lines 21–25) to those of Jaques. What point do you think Shakespeare may have been trying to make? What is your position on the debate?

   c How does Jaques react to the killing of the deer in Act 4 Scene 2? When compared to his earlier reaction, what does his reaction in this scene indicate about Jaques?

3   After Jaques meets Touchstone in the forest, he declares to Duke Senior that he would like to be a "fool" (that is, a court jester) himself. See Act 2 Scene 7 lines 42–43.

   a How does Duke Senior react to Jaques' desire to be a fool?

   b What are Duke Senior's reasons for his reaction?

   c Do you think Duke Senior is justified or not in his reaction? Explain why you think as you do.

4   At the end of the play, Jaques decides not to return to the court with Duke Senior and the others, but instead he joins Duke Frederick, who has decided to become a monk.

   a What does Jaques' decision tell you about him?

   b How does Duke Senior respond to Jaques' decision? What does his response tell you about Duke Senior?

   c Why do you suppose that Shakespeare did not choose to send Jaques back to court with Duke Senior?

Touchstone

Touchstone, the court jester, not only is a source of humor in *As You Like It*, but he also adds depth to the play.

1   Because he is a jester, Touchstone is permitted to say outrageous things that would get other people in trouble if they were to say them.

   a Find examples in the play of things that Touchstone says that the other characters might consider to be outrageous.

   b What general subjects does Touchstone comment about?

   c How do those around him react to his comments?

2   Other characters in the play discuss Touchstone at various times.

   a What are the attitudes of the other characters toward Touchstone?

   b Does he seem to care about what others think of him? Support your answer with examples from the play.

3   A touchstone was a stone used to test the purity of gold or silver. Consequently, when something tests the excellence of something else, it is considered to be a touchstone.

   a Think about Touchstone's relationship to Audrey. What does Touchstone say are his reasons for wanting to marry her?

   b How do his reasons compare and/or contrast with those of the other couples in the play?

   c What is his attitude toward being faithful in marriage? How does his attitude compare to those of the other couples?

   d To what other people or things does Shakespeare use Touchstone and his attitudes as a source of contrast?

4 Think about Touchstone's conversation with Audrey in which he says to her, "[T]he truest poetry is the most feigning" (Act 3 Scene 3 lines 19–20).

   a Explain what Touchstone means by this statement. Do you agree with him or not? Explain why you think as you do about this subject.

   b Compare and contrast Touchstone's mocking poem about Rosalind (see Act 3 Scene 2 lines 101–112) to Orlando's poems about her (see Act 3 Scene 2 lines 88–95 and 125–154). Are any of the ideas or images similar? How do the images differ? Which of the two poems do you think has more validity? Why do you think so?

Themes and Imagery

One of the techniques Shakespeare uses in his plays is to have characters use figurative language to reveal attitudes and emotions or to create an atmosphere. By taking note of repeated ideas or images, we can discover themes which will enhance our understanding of the play.

If the quotation given below is part of a longer speech, read the entire passage in which it appears in order to fully understand what is being said.

Nature versus Fortune

One of the issues Shakespeare invites us to examine in *As You Like It* is to what extent people's lives are affected by what the play refers to as "Nature" and "Fortune." Read and think about these quotes and about which character is speaking the lines.

1.   "Besides this nothing that he so plentifully gives me, the something that nature gave me his countenance seems to take from me. He lets me feed with his hinds, bars me the place of a brother, and, as much as in him lies, mines my gentility with my education."
(Act 1 Scene 1 lines 16–21)

2. "Let us sit and mock the good [housewife] Fortune from her wheel, that her gifts may henceforth be bestow'd equally."
(Act 1 Scene 2 lines 31–33)

3. "Nay, now thou goest from Fortune's office to Nature's. Fortune reigns in gifts of the world, not in the lineaments of Nature."
(Act 1 Scene 2 lines 40–42)

- Shortly after Rosalind and Celia are introduced to the audience, they begin a philosophical discussion about Nature as opposed to Fortune. What do they say about the way Fortune treated women at that time? Do you see anything in their attitudes that seems "modern"? In what ways, if any, do their attitudes seem outdated?

- What aspects of life do the characters in the play believe Nature and Fortune are responsible for? See if you can expand that list. Do you think Nature has more impact now than it did then or vice versa? Why do you think this is the case?

- Based on the events of the play, do you think that Fortune is a more powerful force than Nature or not? Why do you think so?

- Which is more responsible, Nature or Fortune, for the "happy ending" of the play? Explain your reasons for thinking as you do.

- Choose two characters in the play and make a list of the things that Nature and Fortune have given to or done for them. Which seems to dominate each person's life, Nature or Fortune? Compare and contrast the two characters in these respects, and then discuss what you think Shakespeare might have been trying to say about Nature versus Fortune.

Love

There are many references to love in *As You Like It*. Read and think about these quotes and about which character is speaking the lines.

1 "Herein I see thou lov'st me not with the full
   weight that I love thee. If my uncle, thy banish'd
   father, had banished thy uncle, the Duke my
   father, so thou hadst been still with me, I could
   have taught my love to take thy father for mine;
   so wouldst thou, if the truth of thy love to me were
   so righteously temper'd as mine is to thee."
   (Act 1 Scene 2 lines 8–14)

2 "If ever (as that ever may be near)
   You meet in some fresh cheek the power of fancy,
   Then shall you know the wounds invisible
   That love's keen arrows make."
   (Act 3 Scene 5 lines 28–31)

3 "[M]en have died
   from time to time, and worms have eaten them,
   but not for love."
   (Act 4 Scene 1 lines 106–108)

- Find as many other references to love as you can in the play.
- Which characters say they love another character? What kinds of love are depicted in the play?
- What powers does Shakespeare present love as possessing in this play? By what means does he do so?
- What powers does Shakespeare show that love lacks? How does he do so?
- There are several examples of love at first sight in the play, and Phebe utters the quote, "Whoever lov'd that lov'd not at first sight?" (Act 3 Scene 5 line 82). Based on what happens in the play, do you think that Shakespeare believed in love at first sight as a sound basis for a loving relationship?
- Think about quote #3 above. What do you think Rosalind wants to accomplish by her strongly anti-romantic comment?

- What other idea(s) about love do you think Shakespeare was trying to convey in *As You Like It*? How does Shakespeare convey his idea(s) about love?

Life in the Country versus Life in the City

At the time that Shakespeare wrote *As You Like It,* people living in the city or at the royal court tended to view country life as being much simpler and more enjoyable than life in the city. Think about the attitudes that the following quotations reflect.

1   "Now, my co-mates and brothers in exile,
Hath not old custom made this life more sweet
Than that of painted pomp? Are not these woods
More free from peril than the envious court?"
(Act 2 Scene 1 lines 1–4)

2   "Speak you so gently? Pardon me, I pray you.
I thought that all things had been savage here [in the forest],
And therefore put I on the countenance
Of stern command'ment."
(Act 2 Scene 7 lines 106–109)

3   "Truly, shepherd, in respect of itself, it is
a good life; but in respect that it is a shepherd's life,
it is naught. In respect that it is solitary, I like
it very well; but in respect that it is private, it is a
very vild life. Now in respect it is in the fields, it
pleaseth me well; but in respect it is not in the court,
it is tedious."
(Act 3 Scene 2 lines 13–19)

- Think about the events in *As You Like It* that occur in the city (also referred to as being at court). Generally speaking, what is life there like? How do people treat one another?

- What is life like in the forest? How do people treat one another?
- How realistically is life in the forest presented? Do you think that Shakespeare thought that life in the city or life in the country was better? What are your reasons for your opinion?
- Think about which characters remain in the country or forest at the end of the play and which ones return to the court. Discuss their reasons for their decisions. How do their decisions reflect on Shakespeare's examination of life in the country versus life in the city and/or at court?
- What similarities or differences to the values of modern society can you see in this theme?

Deception and Disguise

There are many instances of deception and disguise in *As You Like It*. Read the following quotations and think about the type of deception being discussed.

1   "I came to acquaint
you with a matter. I am given, sir, secretly to
understand that your younger brother, Orlando,
hath a disposition to come in disguis'd against me
to try a fall."
(Act 1 Scene 1 lines 122–126)

2   "I'll put myself in poor and mean attire,
And with a kind of umber smirch my face;
The like do you. So shall we pass along
And never stir assailants."
(Act 1 Scene 3 lines 111–114)

3   "Ah, sirrah, a body
would think this was well counterfeited! I pray
you tell your brother how well I counterfeited.
Heigh-ho!"
(Act 4 Scene 3 lines 165–168)

- Which characters in *As You Like It* deceive others? What
  are their reasons for doing so? Discuss whether any of
  the deceptions seem justified. Do any of them not seem
  justified? Explain your answers.
- Which characters adopt some sort of disguise in the play?
  Why do they do so? Are their reasons helpful or harmful
  to themselves? Are they ever harmful to others?
- Does Shakespeare seem to be making a statement about
  deception in the play? If so, what idea is he trying to
  convey about deception?

Loyalty

Loyalty (sometimes called "love" in the play) is an important
theme in *As You Like It*. Think about the people being discussed
or speaking in the following lines who are showing loyalty to
someone else.

1   "[T]he old Duke is banish'd by his
younger brother the new Duke; and three or
four loving lords have put themselves into voluntary exile with him, whose lands and revenues enrich the new Duke; therefore he gives them good
leave to wander."
(Act 1 Scene 1 lines 99–104)

2   "He'll go along o'er the wide world with me."
(Act 1 Scene 3 line 132)

3 "Master, go on, and I will follow thee
   To the last gasp, with truth and loyalty."
   (Act 2 Scene 3 lines 69–70)

   - Make a list of the characters in the play who show loyalty
     to other characters. What are their reasons for being
     loyal?
   - Are there any instances in the play of social equals being
     loyal to one another, or is the loyalty always given by a
     social inferior to someone higher on the social scale?
   - What ideas, if any, do you think Shakespeare was trying
     to convey about the importance of loyalty in relation-
     ships?

Eyes and Seeing

In Shakespeare's time the eye was an important image, often
used symbolically in paintings, such as in the famous "Rainbow
Portrait" by Isaac Oliver (c. 1600) in which Queen Elizabeth's
cloak is ornamented with eyes and ears in order to show that
she saw and heard everything that happened in her kingdom. (If
you would like to see what this portrait looks like, images are
available on-line. Try searching under "Queen Elizabeth
Rainbow Portrait.")

1 "Young gentleman, your spirits are too bold
   for your years. You have seen cruel proof of this
   man's strength. If you saw yourself with your eyes,
   or knew yourself with your judgment, the
   fear of your adventure would counsel you to a more
   equal enterprise."
   (Act 1 Scene 2 lines 173–177)

2 "If I had a thunderbolt in mine eye, I can tell
   who should down."
   (Act 1 Scene 2 lines 214–215)

3   "Thou tell'st me there is murder in mine eye:
    'Tis pretty, sure, and very probable,
    That eyes, that are the frail'st and softest things,
    Who shut their coward gates on atomies,
    Should be called tyrants, butchers, murtherers!"
    (Act 3 Scene 5 lines 10–14)

- Find as many other references to eyes or the ability to see as you can in the play.
- Which of these refer to literal vision and which refer figuratively to vision or eyes?
- Based on what is said in these references, what idea(s) about eyes or vision do you think Shakespeare was trying to convey?
- Which characters come to see themselves differently during the course of the play? Pick one character and discuss what that character learns about himself or herself.
- Which characters learn to see others differently during the course of the play? Pick one character and discuss what that character learns about another character. Then discuss why the character who has learned to see differently needed to learn to do so.

Animals and Beasts

In *As You Like It*, much of the action occurs in a forest; consequently, it's not surprising that there are many references to animals and beasts. Sometimes the references are general, whereas at other times the characters refer to specific animals.

1   "His horses are bred better, for besides that
      they are fair with their feeding, they are taught
      their manage, and to that end riders dearly hir'd;
      but I (his brother), gain nothing under him but growth,
      for the which his animals on his dunghills are
      as much bound to him as I."
      (Act 1 Scene 1 lines 11–16)

2   "[A] poor sequester'd stag,
      That from the hunter's aim had ta'en a hurt,
      Did come to languish; and indeed, my lord,
      The wretched animal heav'd forth such groans
      That their discharge did stretch his leathern coat
      Almost to bursting, and the big round tears
      Cours'd one another down his innocent nose
      In piteous chase."
      (Act 2 Scene 1 lines 33–40)

3   "I will
      be more jealous of thee than a Barbary cock-
      pigeon over his hen, more clamorous than a parrot
      against rain, more new-fangled than an ape, more
      giddy in my desires than a monkey. I will weep for
      nothing, like Diana in the fountain, and I will do that
      when you are dispos'd to be merry. I will laugh
      like a hyen, and that when thou art inclin'd to sleep."
      (Act 4 Scene 1 lines 149–156)

   • Find other examples of references to animals in *As You
     Like It*. Which ones present animals in a positive way and
     which are negative?

   • What qualities do the animals possess? When these qual-
     ities are being used by the speaker of the lines to reveal
     something about a character, with what aspects of
     human behavior do they deal?

   • What general ideas may Shakespeare have been trying
     to convey in his use of animal imagery?

Examination/Discussion Questions

1. When *As You Like It* was written, boys played the female roles in stage productions because it was considered immoral for a woman to act in public. Consequently, a young male actor would perform the part of Rosalind. Think about watching the play with a boy in Rosalind's role. If you were in the audience in Shakespeare's time, would the fact that a boy was appearing as Rosalind make it harder for you to accept her as a female character? How would it affect the portrayal of Rosalind when she appears as "Ganymede"?

2. Think about the fact that when the play is performed today the role of Rosalind is usually acted by a young woman rather than by a boy. Do you think that modern audiences might find it more difficult than audiences in Shakespeare's time to get caught up in the action of the play, since most of the time that the actress playing Rosalind is on stage, she is pretending to be a boy? Explain your reasons for your opinion.

3. Are there any other aspects of the play that require a "suspension of disbelief" in the audience? That is, are there some aspects of the play that seem difficult to believe and that viewers would have to choose to mentally ignore in order to accept what happens in the play? How much of an obstacle to your enjoyment of the play do these issues present?

4. What does the fact that Rosalind and Celia have a philosophical discussion about Nature and Fortune tell the audience about them? What does their tendency to engage in wordplay such as punning tell you about them?

5   When Le Beau comes to tell Rosalind and Celia about the wrestling match, saying, "There comes an old man and his three sons—," Celia interrupts, saying, "I could match this beginning with an old tale" (Act 1 Scene 2 lines 119–120). In other words, Celia is saying that what Le Beau has said sounds like the beginning of a fairy tale. What aspects of the play remind you of a fairy tale? Do the similarities between *As You Like It* and fairy tales make it difficult to believe the events of the play or not? Explain your reasons for your opinion.

6   When Le Beau invites Rosalind and Celia to watch the wrestling match, Jaques' comments make it clear that watching a wrestling match was not considered to be a socially acceptable form of entertainment for women. Find other examples in the play of the unwritten rules governing appropriate behavior for women at that time. What conclusions can you draw about the way women were viewed? Compare and contrast those views with today's attitudes about women.

7   When Rosalind is banished by Duke Frederick, Celia says, "O my poor Rosalind, whither wilt thou go?" (Act 1 Scene 3 line 90). Although most people think that saying "thee" and "thou" is a very formal way of addressing someone, at the time that Shakespeare wrote *As You Like It*, those were the words used for informal speech, such as when family members or friends spoke to one another. Find other examples in the play in which the characters address one another using the informal mode of address. What do these situations have in common? Do the characters ever say "thee" and "thou" for any purpose other than to speak informally? What other reasons do characters have for using these forms of address?

8 Sometimes, writers include a character that functions as a "foil" to another character. A foil is a character that highlights the good qualities of another character because of the contrast between them. Does Celia function as Rosalind's foil, and, if so, what qualities are contrasted between the two? Do you see any other foils in the play for any of the characters?

9 Compare and contrast the relationships of the men in the play with those of the women. How are they similar? How are they different? Do you think that Shakespeare was trying to show that either gender related to one another better than the other? What are your reasons for your opinion?

10 One of the most famous passages from *As You Like It* is the one that begins with the lines, "All the world's a stage, / and all the men and women merely players." Just as Jaques finishes this speech about the "seven ages" of humanity, Orlando returns carrying Adam (see Act 2 Scene 7 lines 139–166). Compare and contrast the visual image presented by Adam and Orlando to the verbal images that Jaques has just created. Do these images reinforce or undermine each other? Why do you think as you do? What theme or idea, if any, do you think Shakespeare was trying to convey in this situation?

11 When Duke Frederick questions Oliver about where Orlando is, the duke says, "But were I not the better part made mercy, / I should not seek an absent argument / Of my revenge, thou present" (Act 3 Scene 1 lines 2–4). Shakespeare uses the audience's awareness of the fact that Duke Frederick is not at all merciful to create irony. Find other examples of irony in *As You Like It*. Discuss what function these examples perform in the play. In other words, do they reveal character, create humor, increase dramatic tension, or do something else?

12 In one of the poems that Orlando writes about Rosalind, he compares her to other famous females, such as Cleopatra and Helen of Troy (see Act 3 Scene 2 lines 125–154). Find additional instances in which Orlando compares Rosalind to other women. What desirable female qualities do these comparisons highlight? Do you think that Shakespeare was indicating that he agreed with Orlando's notions about the "ideal woman"? Explain why you think as you do.

13 People used to believe that the human body contained four different fluids that determined a person's personality and mood. These fluids were called "humors" and consisted of yellow bile, black bile, phlegm, and blood. People also believed that if these fluids were out of balance illness would result. There are a number of references to humors in *As You Like It.* Find as many of these references as you can, and then think about how Shakespeare incorporates this concept. For example, think about the characters who mention humors. Are they smart or unintelligent, educated or uneducated? Based upon your observations, do you think Shakespeare believed that "humors" affected a person's mood, personality, and health? What are your reasons for thinking as you do?

14 In his poetry, Orlando compares Rosalind to a rare jewel and a beautiful picture (Act 3 Scene 2 lines 88–95). Some Shakespeare scholars believe that thinking of women in terms of inanimate objects such as these reflects a desire by men to "contain rather than affirm female erotic power" (Traub 137). Do you agree with this idea or not? Explain your reasons for your opinion.

15 In a number of instances, events are described by one or more of the characters rather than actually being acted out. Why does Shakespeare choose to present these

events verbally rather than visually? Do you think he was trying to emphasize some idea about the power of vision or do you think he had some other reason for presenting the scenes as he does?

16 When Rosalind, disguised as "Ganymede," has a conversation with Jaques, she tells him, "Those that are in extremity of either are / abominable fellows, and betray themselves to every / modern censure worse than drunkards" (Act 4 Scene 1 lines 5–7). Her statement to Jaques reflects the concept of maintaining the "golden mean," as proposed by Aristotle, which meant that one should strive to avoid going to extremes in behavior or emotion. What are the benefits of such an idea? Are there drawbacks, and, if so, what are they?

17 According to Margaret Loftus Ranald, by the time Rosalind and Orlando wed, Orlando "has been educated into an acceptance of Rosalind's view of love in which sexuality is an important component" (73). Find examples from the play in which Rosalind (as "Ganymede") teaches Orlando that sexuality is a part of a loving marital relationship. Why would she consider it important for him to recognize and accept this concept?

18 When Orlando comes upon Duke Senior and his followers in the forest, he tries to force them to give him food for Adam, but Duke Senior replies, "What would you have? Your gentleness shall force, / More than your force move us to gentleness" (Act 2 Scene 7 lines 101–102). Explain what you think this scene says about the issue of power.

19 In addition to physical violence, what other forms of power can you see in the play? What ideas concerning power might Shakespeare be trying to convey in *As You Like It*?

20 At one time, if a man's wife was unfaithful to him and the community found out about it, he would be called a "cuckold." According to tradition, in some European villages, people would force the man to wear horns or antlers on his head and he would be marched through the town in a ceremony of public humiliation. Find as many references to cuckolding in *As You Like It* as you can. What cultural attitudes do these references reflect? What fears do they reveal?

21 In Act 4 Scene 2, the lords sing a song about the horns of the deer. Compare this situation to the idea of cuckolding as described in question #20. Are the horns mentioned in the song entirely positive, or does the song seem to have negative implications as well, considering the social implications of wearing horns at that time?

22 Shakespeare includes a number of songs in *As You Like It*. What function do these songs perform? For example, do they move the plot forward? Do they reveal things about the characters? Do they comment on the themes of the play?

23 In the drama of ancient Greece, a god would appear to unravel all the difficulties that had arisen; this god was called the *deus ex machina*. Any artificial solution (now referred to in general as a *deus ex machina*, even when an actual god is not involved) is now considered to be an inferior way to deal with plot complications. At the end of *As You Like It*, the god of weddings, Hymen, appears to bless the marriages of the four couples. Does he function as a *deus ex machina*? Explain your reasons for your answer. Then think about other aspects of the end of the play. Do you see any artificial or overly convenient solutions to complications in the play?

24 When Rosalind reappears at the end of the play for the wedding, she says to both her father and to Orlando, "To thee I give myself, for I am yours" (Act 5 Scene 4 lines 116–117). Does the fact that she says she belongs to these two men reduce her to an object to be possessed? What are your reasons for your opinion?

25 Think about the four couples who marry at the end of *As You Like It*. Compare and contrast the four relationships. What would you say is the basis of each one? That is, what was the primary reason for each couple being united? What ideas about love and marriage do you think Shakespeare was trying to convey through these contrasting characters?

Sources

Barber, C. L. "The Alliance of Seriousness and Levity." *Modern Critical Interpretations: William Shakespeare's "As You Like It."* Ed. Harold Bloom. New York: Chelsea, 1988. 5–21.

Barton, Ann. "*As You Like It*: Essay." *The Riverside Shakespeare.* 2nd ed. Boston: Houghton Mifflin, 1997. 399–402.

Berry, Wendell. "The Uses of Adversity." *Sewanee Review* 115.2 (2007): 211–223.

Bloom, Harold. *Shakespeare: The Invention of the Human.* New York: Riverhead, 1998.

Leach, Robert. "*As You Like It*: A 'Robin Hood' Play." *English Studies* 82.5 (2001): 393–400.

Ranald, Margaret Loftus. *Shakespeare and His Social Context.* New York: AMS, 1987.

Ronk, Martha. "Locating the Visual in *As You Like It*." *Shakespeare Quarterly* 52.2 (2001): 255–310.

Traub, Valerie. "Jewels, Statues, and Corpses: Containment of Female Erotic Power in Shakespeare's Plays." *Shakespeare and Gender: A History.* Ed. Deborah Barker and Ivo Kamps. London: Verso, 1995. 120–141.

Wells Slights, Camille. "Pastoral and Parody in *The Merry Wives of Windsor*." *English Studies in Canada* 11.1 (1985): 12–25.

Scene 7

Macbeth's castle. Enter a **sewer** *directing divers servants. Then enter* **Macbeth.**

Macbeth If it were done, when 'tis done, then 'twere well
It were done quickly: if th' assassination
Could trammel up the consequence, and catch,
With his surcease, success; that but this blow
5 Might be the be-all and the end-all here,
But here, upon this bank and shoal of time,
We'd jump the life to come. But in these cases
We still have judgement here: that we but teach
Blood instructions, which being taught return
10 To plague th'inventor: this even-handed justice
Commends th'ingredience of our poisoned chalice
To our own lips. He's here in double trust:
First, as I am his kinsman and his subject,
Strong both against the deed: then, as his host,
15 Who should against his murderer shut the door,
Not bear the knife myself. Besides, this Duncan
Hath borne his faculties so meek, hath been
So clear in his great office, that his virtues
Will plead like angels, trumpet-toungèd, against
20 The deep damnation of his taking-off;
And pity, like a naked new-born babe,
Striding the blast, or Heaven's cherubin, horsed
Upon the sightless couriers of the air,
Shall blow the horrid deed in every eye,
25 That tears shall drown the wind. I have no spur
To prick the sides of my intent, but only
Vaulting ambition, which o'erleaps itself,
And falls on th'other –

Scene 7

A room in **Macbeth's** *castle. A* **Butler** *and several* **Waiters** *cross, carrying dishes of food. Then* **Macbeth** *enters. He is thinking about the proposed murder of* **King Duncan.**

Macbeth If we could get away with the deed after it's done, then the quicker it were done, the better. If the murder had no consequences, and his death ensured success...If, when I strike the blow, that would be the end of it – here, right here, on this side of eternity – we'd willingly chance the life to come. But usually, we get what's coming to us here on earth. We teach the art of bloodshed, then become the victims of our own lessons. This evenhanded justice makes us swallow our own poison. [*Pause*] Duncan is here on double trust: first, because I'm his kinsman and his subject (both good arguments against the deed); then, because I'm his host, who should protect him from his murderer—not bear the knife. Besides, this Duncan has used his power so gently, he's been so incorruptible his great office, that his virtues will plead like angels, their tongues trumpeting the damnable horror of his murder. And pity, like a naked newborn babe or Heaven's avenging angels riding the winds, will cry the deed to everyone so that tears will blind the eye. I've nothing to spur me on but high-leaping ambition, which can often bring about one's downfall.